A Princely Gift:

The Rudy Lamont Ruggles Collection
of
The Newberry Library

Rudy Lamont Ruggles

A Princely Gift:

The Rudy Lamont Ruggles Collection
of
The Newberry Library

Compiled by
Richard Colles Johnson and Cynthia H. Peters

Introduction by
Lawrence W. Towner

The Newberry Library, 1986
Chicago

Copyright ©1986 by The Newberry Library

Printed in The United States of America
by
R. R. Donnelley & Sons Company

ISBN 0-911028-35-8

PREFACE

Although the Ruggles Collection is too large to be shown at one time, it is expected that all of it eventually will be on display in one context or another. What follows, therefore, has been designed as an exhibition catalogue: one meant to be read, which we hope will prove enjoyable to the viewer, the reader, and the ultimate user. While we have eschewed technical bibliographical symbols and references to specific bibliographies, the standard bibliographies have of course been freely used, and the identification of editions, issues, and states has been noted where appropriate. Also mentioned are instances of notable condition, bindings, and association copies, of which there are a very considerable number.

The catalogue is alphabetical by author or corporate entry ("Great Britain. Laws"; "United States. Continental Congress"); within each entry the order is chronological. American presidents have been entered under their names instead of under "United States. President."

For what errors there may be we can only apologize, not only to the reader, but also to Mr. Ruggles, whose collection it has been a pleasure to describe.

Richard Colles Johnson
Cynthia H. Peters

INTRODUCTION

"The trouble with lawyers," wrote David A. Randall of The Scribner Book Store in October 1949, "is that they have to work all the time . . . to get enough money to buy books." In that one sentence, he neatly summed up two very important if unequal aspects of the life of his new acquaintance and soon-to-be friend, Rudy Lamont Ruggles of Chicago. In 1949 Mr. Ruggles was already well on his way to recognition as an outstanding lawyer who happened to collect books. Now, with the publication of this catalogue, his reputation becomes that of an outstanding book collector who happens to have practiced law. The Newberry Library is the happy beneficiary of this shift.

In truth, of course, there is no incompatability between the two vocations, except that the practice of law ordinarily does take a lot of time away from being a collector. But in this case, the practice of law reinforced the Collector. It gave him foreknowledge of a major aspect of the collection he was forming—early American law, particularly constitutional law and the adoption of the Constitution of the United States.

This princely gift goes well beyond the Constitution and American Law, however. It is a collection of collections, and it joins a library that has been quite appropriately characterized by the happy phrase, "An Uncommon Collection of Uncommon Collections." So the Ruggles library adds its name to a long list of important collections that have been coming to the Library, by gift or purchase, since even before the Newberry opened its doors in 1893. The earliest ones purchased were the Pio Resse in music history and theory, the Probasco collection of rare books and fine bindings, the Louis Lucien Bonaparte in linguistics, and the Main in English and American psalmody—all by 1891; the earliest major gift, in 1911, was that of Edward E. Ayer.

More than that, the Ruggles Collection joins the much shorter list of Newberry's Special Collections gathered, given, and *endowed* by the Collectors: Edward E. Ayer (1911); John M. Wing (1919); William B. Greenlee (1937); and Everett D. Graff (1964). Each of these Special Collections is separately catalogued, separately shelved (rather than interfiled), served under careful supervision in the Rare Book Reading Room, and separately endowed for continued growth. Even before the Ruggles Collection became a gift, on 19 December 1985, Mr. Ruggles' wife Ruth Cain Ruggles had started an endowment fund at the Library for that purpose.

A focal point of the Ruggles Collection on the Constitution is Thomas Jefferson's own copy of that great American political commentary, *The Federalist* (116), bound in contemporary calf, with Jefferson's penned attributions of authorship amongst Hamilton, Jay, and Madison. To hold these volumes is to touch hands with Mr. Jefferson. (There is only one other known book from Jefferson's Library in the Newberry, the Graff copy of Lewis and Clark's *History of the Expedition*.) With the Jefferson *Federalist* is the 1829 sale catalogue of his library (286). These works are handsomely complemented by the manuscript of *Federalist* essay number three in John Jay's own hand (190). Out of the eighty-five essays, only four manuscripts survive, all in Jay's hand. This is one of them.

Closely-related works include: the 1784 broadside of the Continental Congress (350) concerning the need for control over trade; a splendid and most interesting letter on the convention itself, Madison to Noah Webster, 12 October 1804 (238); three other copies of the first book edition of *The Federalist* (115, 117, 118) in a different condition and/or with a different association; thirty-three of the various original newspaper printings of the individual *Federalist* essays (114), gathered by William Cushing (of whom more later); and Washington's letter to Jay, thanking him for the presentation copy of volume one of *The Federalist* sent shortly after publication (363).

On the adoption of the Constitution, see also the *Debates* of the crucial Virginia ratifying convention (356) and a pro-Federalist essay by Jonathan Jackson (188) printed by Isaiah Thomas, the patriot printer, whose *History of Printing in America* is also in the collection (332). The Constitution itself is present in its first magazine appearance, the very month of September 1787 that it was submitted to the states for ratification (69), and in the first London edition of that year (343).

The amendments that became the Bill of Rights are the substance of: a newspaper story from Madison, attached to Jefferson's *Federalist*; of the *Gazette of the United States'* (136) publication of the debates in the House and Senate on the Amendments; and of the official Senate *Journal* (342), all in the collection. Earlier on, Virginia had provided a strong impetus for the Bill of Rights in her ratifying convention (356). And, as background for the First Amendment, the collection provides John Milton's *Areopagitica* (258), and three items on John Peter Zenger, whose case in New York City in the mid-eighteenth century concerned freedom of the press—the pamphlet and the newspaper (382, 268, and see also 267).

The adoption of the proposed frame of government—a government that includes the rest of what became the United States largely because of the Northwest Ordinance (352, 390, 391)—was the climax of an intensive period of constitution-making in America from 1776 to 1789. It can be said that the process, especially ratification by representatives chosen for that purpose, was virtually an American invention. Thus, in what historian Robert R. Palmer has called *The Age of Revolution,* Europe developed a strong interest in American constitution-making.

As early as 1781, the Congress under the Articles of Confederation caused a volume to be printed with the *Constitutions of the Several Independent States of America* (70, 71), which includes the newly-adopted Articles of Confederation and other documents. Then began a great diplomatic venture by Benjamin Franklin, who had the work translated for publication in Paris. The Ruggles copies of the French edition include an uncut copy (72), a thick paper copy, partially unopened and in original wrappers (73), and the large-paper issue (74), one of several on special paper and one of six bound in morocco, which were for special presentation. The collection also includes John Adams' *Defence of the Constitutions of Government of the United States* (3), published in London, the first volume of which reached the United States in time to contribute to the debates over the Constitution.

Another cluster of documents on the Constitution, after its adoption, has as its focus John Jay's manuscript commission as first Chief Justice of the Supreme Court of the United States, signed by George Washington (364). Jay later resigned to become Governor of New York, and President John Adams, at the end of his presidency, sought to reappoint him to the Court. Jay declined and returned the commission: the collection has Adams's and Secretary of State John Marshall's letters to Jay and Jay's letters of refusal (4, 245, 191, 192). The upshot was the appointment of John Marshall.

The emphasis placed here so far on the Constitutional Period should not obscure the fact that the collection contains a large number of other books "important in the development of American history," as Mr. Ruggles described it in 1972. A few examples will illustrate the point: Jay's Treaty (353), Washington's Farewell Address (365), The Monroe Doctrine (262); the *American Scholar* (109); Davy Crockett (88), the Audubon (13, 14); the Lincoln-Douglas Debates (98); The Gettysburg Address (112); The Emancipation Proclamation (225); Lee's Surrender at Appomattox (219); and *The Education of Henry Adams* (2). But more important than individual items is a series of focussed collections.

One in that series is *Illinois History,* which will provide the basis for many significant exhibitions. There are more than fifty important works in this field, including several pre-Chicago-fire imprints, six books by early Governor John Reynolds (294–299), the 1818 and later constitutions (181–183), Breese's important *Cases 1819–1830* (38), Beck's *Gazetteer* 1823 (22), Burlend's *A*

True Picture (49), Regan's *Emigrant's Guide* of 1852 (293), John Woods' *Two Years' Residence* (381), and Peck's *Guide* (275) and *Gazetteer* (276), to pick several important works quite arbitrarily. On Chicago alone, there are some twenty interesting works. Two concern the Fort Dearborn "massacre" of 1812 (209, 213); there follow Guyer's *Chicago* (147) and the *Fergus Historical Series* (119); two provide before and after views of the Great Fire, the important Frignet and Carrey work, with its ten pre-fire photographic scenes (135), and its almost-companion piece, three years after the fire, Chamberlin (53), both accompanied by the famous Chicago *Evening Journal—Extra,* October 9, 1871 (111) the day after the fire began; and, finally, not to be overlooked, is the 1886 Haymarket Riot broadside, *Attention Workingmen!* (12).

High spots from the *American Revolution* are also well represented, from the hated and incendiary 1765 Stamp Act (143) and Franklin's testimony in Parliament against it (129), to the manuscript instructions for the American commissioners in Europe, 1782, ordering them not to make a separate peace with Britain (349). They include a Boston Tea Party broadside 1773 (35); Alexander Hamilton's first publication, 1774, in favor of the colonies (150); Hancock's address in 1775 commemorating the Boston Massacre and keeping its memory green (151); the Continental Congress' 1774 "Declaration of Rights" (345); its 1775 declaration of "Causes for Taking Up Arms" (346, 347); the first English and first American editions of Burke's speech on *Conciliation* (45–47); Paine's *Common Sense,* clearing the ideological way for revolution, first printing, 1776 (272); and the first magazine printing of the Declaration of Independence (278). On the military side, the "Holster Atlas" for British officers (9); Simcoe's *Queen's Rangers,* a Loyalist force (311); military accounts of the two main British generals Clinton and Cornwallis and their controversy (64, 65, 76, and 66—with copious Clinton manuscript notes); and Bannastre Tarleton's military account (327) are all present.

Also of patriotic interest are the Ruggles items on the *Star-Spangled Banner.* Unless one were an expert, he might easily miss their importance. Here is the first printing, in London, of the music, circa 1780: the "Anacreontic Song" (338) as sung at the Crown and Anchor Tavern in the Strand, to whose music, some thirty years later, Francis Scott Key's "Star Spangled Banner" was set. The words alone appeared under the title the "Defence of Fort M'Henry" in Baltimore (203), Philadelphia (204), Hagerstown (205), and elsewhere; and, finally, the *Star Spangled Banner,* with words and music, appears in this collection in the first New York edition (206). "The Liberty Song," published in the Boston *Chronicle* for 26 December 1768 (34), is a precursor, for it was the first American patriotic song. It was written by John Dickinson and sung to the English tune "Hearts of Oak." All the above fit nicely with the first printing of the Great Seal of the United States in a book (72); and the first printing, in color, of the American flag (170) in a German work on the American Revolution, published in 1784.

Works on the *American Indian*—at least seventeen are here, from Thomas Harriot's *Virginiae* (153), with the famous de Bry engravings based on John White's sixteenth-century drawings and watercolors from the lost Roanoke colony, on up to Karl Bodmer's splendid nineteenth-century portfolio in Maximilian of Wied's *Travels, 1843–44* (372). They include Roger Williams' *Key into the Language of America,* 1643 (374), English legislation, 1649, establishing the Corporation for the Propagation of the Gospel among the Indians in New England (141), as well as two important Indian captivity narratives, Rowlandson (303) in the seventeenth century and Jemison (308) in the nineteenth.

Early American Maps also have a place in this collection. At least fifteen important works are included, from Champlain's *Voyages* (54), with the important and often missing map, and Joutel's *Journal* (200), both on French America, to the rare and complete Christopher Colles, *Roads of the United States* (68), an amazing series of strip maps of the Eastern United States in 1789. Also present are Lewis and Clark's *Expedition* (222); and Frémont's *Report* (134), with their maps of the Far West; and such important maps as the "Holster Atlas" (9), Evans (110), Hutchins (179), Mitchell (259), and Pownall (288), among others.

American and English literature are also well represented, old friends by authors from William Cullen Bryant to Hemingway, from Shakespeare to Joyce—that we recognize and delight in. *The Raven* (284), *Nature* (107), *Walden* (334), *Leaves of Grass* (369), *Two Years before the Mast* (86), *Huckleberry Finn* (62), *The Luck of Roaring Camp* (157), and *Moby-Dick* (257), all in splendid condition, are matched in English literature by the *Faerie Queen* (317), *Peregrine Pickle* (315), Pepys' *Diary* (280), *A Tale of a Tub* (323), *Tristram Shandy* (321), *Emma* (15), *Alice* (95), *Ulysses* (201), and others, *all in superb condition.*

There are several important works in this collection that have thus far escaped categorization and, therefore, mention. They will, of course, reveal themselves to the careful reader of the catalogue. Even so, the temptation to list a few is irresistible. The earliest work is the thirteenth-century Latin *Bible,* a beautiful manuscript (26). But there are other important religious works, such as the leaf from the Gutenberg *Bible* (27); the Aitken *Bible* (25), the *Book of Mormon* (313), and Mary Baker Eddy's *Science and Health* (103). Of different kinds of importance are early reference works such as Bowditch's *New American Practical Navigator* (37), Webster's *Dictionary* (367), Bartlett's *Quotations* (20), and Bulfinch's *Age of Fable* (44). Some beauties are Bewick's *Birds*

(24), Bligh's *Mutiny* (33), Fletcher's *Russe Common Wealth* (122), Gower's *Confessione* (140), and Fraunce's *Lawiers Logike* (133). Finally, there are a few books that are simply important: Darwin's *Origin of Species* (87), Keynes' *General Theory of Employment* (207), Mahan's *Sea Power* (240), Malthus' *Political Economy* (241), and, a sleeper, Smyth's *Atomic Energy* (316). There are more!

Another dozen subjects suggest themselves when the catalogue is reviewed. Small but good exhibits can be mounted on *Benjamin Franklin, Alexander Hamilton, John Jay, Thomas Jefferson,* and *George Washington.* In addition to several items under Washington's name, there are the famous funeral sermon by Henry Lee: "First in war, first in peace, and first in the hearts of his countrymen" (218); and the *Book of Common Prayer* (292) believed to have been used by Washington. Exhibition materials are also present for such topics as *Dickens at Christmas Time, Children's Literature, Travel Narratives, Illustrated Books, The Old Northwest, Early American Science and Medicine, Local Colorists,* and *American Law.*

Law, as a matter of fact, and not just constitutional law, is important in this collection, as is quite evident in the catalogue. Early Massachusetts law (247–251), the Zenger case (382), legal commentaries (31, 32, 202), Breese's *Illinois Cases* (38), and Holmes' *Common Law* (173–174) come immediately to mind. Less obvious (and not noted in the catalogue) is the fact that many of the collection's authors were trained in the law, enough of them to mount an interesting exhibit on Literary Lawyers; and certainly our donor, Rudy Lamont Ruggles, can be considered a literary lawyer himself.

As for his motivation to collect in many fields, he notes that early in his career, even as an undergraduate, he had decided that the pleasure of reading in the original such a masterwork as Cotton Mather's *Magnalia Christi Americana* (London 1702) far outmatched reading, say, *Gulliver's Travels* or even *The Federalist* in modern paperback editions. Therefore he started to seek out such original works as the two fine copies of Mather's *Magnalia,* first edition, in the collection (253, 254). They well illustrate his desire to have in his own library "copies of certain books in their *original state or in some contemporary, associative, or otherwise meaningful condition."* (Emphasis added).

With those criteria developed, and with Jefferson's wonderful copy of the *Federalist* in hand, there was no way he could resist purchasing a splendid work offered in June 1962 by David A. Randall. It was William Cushing's *Federalist* scrapbook, the first appearance of thirty-three of the essays, in newspapers, gathered by Cushing (114). Enough reason to buy, right there. But reasons abounded.

Cushing was a descendant of John Cotton, that major figure in early Massachusetts theological and political history and Cotton Mather's grandfather. As a judge, Cushing himself had found in the famous 1783 Quock Walker case in Massachusetts that the state's Declaration of Rights prohibited slavery. George Washington later appointed Cushing as the first Associate Justice of the Supreme Court of the United States. On Jay's absence in England to negotiate what became known as Jay's Treaty, Cushing served as acting Chief Justice and, in that capacity, administered the oath of office at Washington's second inaugural. He subsequently turned down Washington's proffer of the chief justiceship. "Contemporary, associative, or otherwise meaningful condition," indeed!

Condition was always a major concern of Mr. Ruggles, and the books in this collection are in *superb* physical condition. For example, the presence of duplicates, besides choices made because of association, also reveals additions made to improve condition. Duplicates include, among others: Dana's *Two Years before the Mast* (85, 86); Clemens' *Huckleberry Finn* (62, 63); Franklin's Paris edition of the *Constitutions* (72–74); Franklin's *Memoirs* (130, 131); Hawthorne's *Mosses from an Old Manse* (160, 161) and the *Scarlet Letter* (162, 163); Holmes' *Common Law* (173, 174); and Markham's *The Man with the Hoe* (243, 244). But one duplicate, unfortunately did not come to the Newberry as part of our "Princely Gift."

Mr. Ruggles once owned two copies of the first American edition of *Moby-Dick* (New York, 1851), one of them in a red binding that was greatly coveted by the Lilly Library. In the single known instance of an exchange, Mr. Ruggles traded it, very reluctantly, for a copy of Mary Rowlandson's Indian captivity narrative (303), which now has the distinguished modern provenance of Helen Gody Wilson, Bernardo Mendel, Lathrop Harper, the Lilly Library, Rudy L. Ruggles, and The Newberry Library. Despite the facts that the *Moby-Dick* was a "duplicate," except for the color of the binding, and that the Rowlandson was not yet in the Ruggles Collection, some pain accompanied this transaction. In the end, friendship prevailed, for at the Lilly, as Director, was David A. Randall, who had, over the years, been so helpful in assembling the collection. Later, when Mr. Rudy Ruggles, Jr., had occasion to lunch in Bloomington as the guest of honor of University Chancellor Herman B Wells, there, on the table in front of him was the red *Moby-Dick*.

The well-known and long-term friendship that developed over the years between Randall and Rudy Ruggles as bookmen—illuminated by the Rowlandson/Melville swap—should not lead one to assume that Randall was Ruggles' only supplier of rare books. The *Moby-Dick* had been sold to him by Harold Graves, later associated with Scribner's, when Graves was still at Kroch's and

Brentano's in Chicago. Mr. Ruggles also bought from Philip Duschnes, Edward Eberstadt & Sons, and Arthur Swann in New York, for examples; and, in Chicago, from Arthur Halperin of George Chandler's Bookstore, Hamill and Barker, the Central Book Store, and Kenneth Nebenzahl, Inc., among others.

But certainly, Randall was the most influential supplier. He wore well. As early as 28 July 1949, he had written "Mr. Ruggles" that "Our mutual friend Harold Greenhill [the late Chicago collector, some of whose books are now in this collection] has told me that you are interested in rare books. . . ."

Sixteen years later, on 14 April 1965, long after "Mr. Ruggles" had given way to "Dear Rudy," Randall could still expect resistance against suggestions for adding to the collection, especially but by no means exclusively for expensive items, in this case the Jay Commission (364) signed by Washington. "I know it is tax day tomorrow . . ." Randall wrote, "there always will be—but there is only one document of our First President appointing our first Supreme Court Chief-Justice." The argument was irresistible. Once Mr. Ruggles had bought the document and had it cleaned, he had it framed according to the best conservation techniques available, at the now defunct "Extra Bindery" at R. R. Donnelley & Sons Company by the famed Harold Tribolet—who did many tasks for this collection.

In becoming the kind of a collector to whom internationally-known book dealers would offer the kinds of high spots Mr. Ruggles put in his collection, he recalls, he systematically "visited bookshops and perused their stocks, requested catalogues, watched the items put up at auction both in New York and London, and noted the prices they fetched. I read books about book-collecting and books about books. I talked with book-collectors and other men of bookish interest whenever I had the opportunity. Perhaps the most pleasant and fruitful way of sharpening my technical knowledge was through the exchange of ideas with good booksellers, some of whom were invaluable as tutors. Bit by bit I was able to try my wings, and as my accumulating took on larger and more important proportions, it progressed to a point . . . where what I had gathered became referred to as a collection." Yes, and the owner of it, a bookman, a Collector.

Over the course of many years, as the Collector and The Newberry Library discussed the Ruggles Collection and the appropriateness of its coming to the Newberry, other possible recipients inevitably came to mind. Any library in the country would be delighted to have it. Several let that fact be known. But the Collector decided he wanted to place it in Chicago, and quite naturally he chose the Newberry, where he has served as Trustee since 1964. Finally, when Trustee and old friend Rudy L. Ruggles decided to present his Collection to the Newberry on 19 December

1985, the Trustees, of course, accepted with great pleasure, alacrity, and acclaim. It fit the Newberry's Uncommon Collections so very well!

I, of course, was absolutely delighted that this collection, this splendid collection, this uncommon collection, this special collection, should come to The Newberry Library in my last year as Librarian. The gift was a special act of particular generosity, and I know it. So it is that I have the pleasure, on behalf of the present generation of scholars who already use the collection and of the future generations who shall use it, of thanking Mr. Ruggles and his family, Mrs. Ruggles, Rudy, Jr., and Jean—who all supported his decision to make this princely gift. It will be here as long as forever lasts.

Lawrence W. Towner

Chicago, July 9, 1986

1. **[HENRY ADAMS]**
   Democracy: An American Novel.
   New York: Henry Holt, 1880.

   Adams's first novel was submitted to his friend Henry Holt in the spring of 1879 under "a pledge of dead secrecy," and the book was published anonymously a year later. The secret of authorship was kept until 1915 when it was disclosed by William Roscoe Thayer. The book gives a picture of Washington life in the late 1870's. This copy is the first printing and binding, and as such, very rare.

2. **[HENRY ADAMS]**
   The Education of Henry Adams.
   Washington, 1907.

   At the Paris Exhibition of 1900 Adams saw the huge dynamo that he was to take as a symbol of mechanistic power and energy of the multiplicity of the twentieth century, as contrasted to the unity (symbolized by the Virgin) of the thirteenth century. He wrote *Mont St. Michel and Chartres* (1904) to describe the latter, and his classic *Education* to describe the former, which he called "a study of twentieth-century multiplicity." It was printed in an edition of perhaps one hundred copies in 1907 and not issued commercially until after his death, when it appeared in a revised form. This copy, in the original blue binding, is unopened.

3. **JOHN ADAMS**
   A Defence of the Constitutions of Government of the United States of America.
   London: C. Dilly, 1787.

   Written when the author was American envoy to the Court of St. James's, the first volume of Adams's *Defence* appeared in America while the convention for framing a constitution was assembling. Its timeliness gave it vogue and it was immediately put to use, but it is chiefly remembered for the unjustifiable partisan interpretation given to it in later years as an attempt to favor a monarchy. Two further volumes, dealing with the history of the Italian republics, were added later. This copy is inscribed "Dr Thomas Wren, from the Author." The recipient was a dissenting minister in Portsmouth who administered relief to Americans in prison during the Revolution and who received an honorary doctorate from the College of New Jersey at Franklin's instigation.

4. **JOHN ADAMS**
   A.L.S. to John Jay.
   Washington, 19 December 1800. 2 pp.

   Upon the resignation of Oliver Ellsworth from the office of Chief Justice of the Supreme Court, President Adams sent this letter to Jay advising him of his renomination to that office. At the time Jay was serving his second term as Governor of New York, and Adams writes, "You may very properly resign the short remainder of your gubernatorial period." Having lost the Presidential election to Jefferson in the fall of 1800, Adams was anxious to have another Federalist replace Ellsworth before the Republican President was inaugurated. Jay's letter declining this office is also in the collection, as is the exchange of letters on the same subject between John Marshall (then Secretary of State) and Jay.

5. **JOHN QUINCY ADAMS**
   Report upon Weights and Measures.
   Washington: Gales & Seaton, 1821.

   Adams, who had a high regard for science, prepared this *Report* while Secretary of State. Compiled over four years, it is a study of weights and measures in the several states and in foreign countries for the purpose of establishing uniformity and became the basis for United States federal standards. This copy, printed on thick paper, is inscribed to John Jay.

6. **JOHN QUINCY ADAMS**
   The Jubilee of the Constitution.
   New York: Samuel Colman, 1839.

   Adams, who had been the sixth President of the United States, delivered this discourse at the request of the New-York Historical Society on "the fiftieth anniversary of the inauguration of George Washington as President of the United States on Thursday, the 30th of April, 1789." This copy is inscribed on the front wrapper from the author to the Rev. John Sibley, who was later to compile "Sibley's *Harvard Graduates.*"

7. **THOMAS BAILEY ALDRICH**
   The Story of a Bad Boy.
   Boston: Fields, Osgood, 1870.

   Aldrich was born in Portsmouth, New Hampshire, the scene of his semi-autobiographical novel. It has been called the first realistic American juvenile and, with *Hans Brinker* (1866) and *Little Women* (1868), one of the first three great American children's

Washington Dec'r 19 1800

Dear Sir

Mr Elsworth afflicted with the Gravel and the Gout in his Kidneys, and intending to pass the Winter in the South of France after a few Weeks in England, has resigned his Office of Chief Justice, and I have nominated you to your old Station. This is as independent of the Inclination of the People as his of the Will of a President. In the future Administration of our Country the firmest Security we can have against the Effects of visionary Schemes or fluctuating Theories, will be in a Solid Judiciary: and nothing will cheer the hopes of the best Men so much as your Acceptance of this appointment. You have now a great opportunity to render a most signal Service to your Country. I therefore pray you most earnestly to consider of it, seriously and accept it. You may very properly resign the Short Remainder of your Gubernatorial Period, and Mr Van Rensselaer may discharge the Duties. I had no permission from you to take this Step, but it appeared to me that Providence had thrown in my way an Opportunity, not only of marking to the Public the Spot where, in my opinion, the greatest Mass of Worth remained collected in one Individual, but of furnishing my Country with the best Security, its

---

4. John Adams, A.L.S. to John Jay (1800)

books. Aldrich went on to write acclaimed poetry and stories, but this book is his lasting achievement. The present copy is of the first state.

8. **HORATIO ALGER, JR.**
Ragged Dick; or, Street Life in New York with the Boot-blacks.
Boston: Loring, [1868]

Two years in the ministry were enough for Alger, and in 1866 he moved to New York City and lived at the Newsboys' Lodging, where his warm heart and sympathetic manner won the confidence of its inmates. They provided him with the plots of many of his 119 books, of which *Ragged Dick* was the first to become famous. His "rags-to-riches" stories, where virtue is always rewarded by wealth and honor, became a hallmark of American lore. This copy is of the first issue.

9. *The American Military Pocket Atlas . . .*
London: R. Sayer and J. Bennett, [1776]

After the beginning of the Revolution, the London map publishers Sayer and Bennett issued these maps, which the British high command regarded as providing essential topographical information in the most convenient form. The atlas, known as the "Holster Atlas" because British officers carried it in their holsters, comprises six large folding maps showing the colonies "which now are, or probably may be, the theatre of war." The maps (North America, West Indies, Northern Colonies, Middle Colonies, Southern Colonies, Lake Champlain) are large-scale general reference maps, and the work is dedicated to Thomas Pownall, member of Parliament and former Governor of Massachusetts, at whose recommendation it was compiled. This copy contains the maps laid in loose in a case, as issued.

10. **BENEDICT ARNOLD**
Proceedings of a General Court Martial of the Line . . .
Philadelphia: Francis Bailey, 1780.

George Washington ordered this court-martial to inquire into alleged irregularities during General Arnold's command in Philadelphia in 1778, a court-martial which Arnold himself demanded. It started on 19 December 1779 at a tavern in Morristown, New Jersey, where Washington and his troops were spending the winter; Arnold was acquitted of the two major charges but judged censurable on two minor ones—carelessness regarding shipping and use of troops for personal purposes. It was not known that he was already in correspondence with Sir Henry Clinton, which led to Arnold's treachery and flight the following year. Only fifty copies of this official edition of the court-martial were printed; this one is in its original wrappers and bears the signature of William Floyd, one of the signers of the Declaration of Independence from New York.

11. **TIMOTHY SHAY ARTHUR**
Ten Nights in a Bar-Room, and What I Saw There.
Boston: L. P. Crown; Philadelphia: J. W. Bradley, 1854.

Arthur was a prolific and popular journalist and novelist. This book became the literary spearhead of the temperance movement in America, with a sale in the fifties and sixties second only to *Uncle Tom's Cabin.* It was sensational and lurid and yet, at the same time, the clergy endorsed it, making it one book of fiction that young Americans might safely read on Sunday. Arthur by his pen achieved as much for the temperance movement as others did from the lecture platform. This copy has the earlier form of the frontispiece and is in unusually fine condition for a book which was generally read to tatters.

12. *Attention Workingmen! Great Mass Meeting To-night...*
[Chicago, 1886]

The Haymarket Riot of 4 May 1886 grew out of labor strikes in Chicago for an eight-hour working day. A street meeting, called by delegates of the unions to protest the killing of a striker the day before, led to the Riot. A bomb thrown into the police units killed seven, a panic ensued, and the eventual trial sentenced seven laborites to death, of whom four were executed. This edition of the broadside calling the meeting omits the provocative words "Workingmen arm yourselves and appear in full force" and has the third line of the German text in roman type.

13. **JOHN JAMES AUDUBON**
The Birds of America.
New York: J. J. Audubon; Philadelphia: J. B. Chevalier, 1840–44. 7 vols.

The first American octavo edition of Audubon's great folio *Birds of America* (1827–1838) was published in one hundred parts and sold to subscribers between 1840 and 1844 at $100. Compared to the original cost of the four elephant folio volumes of the *Birds* at $1,000, the "miniature edition" was more affordable—in fact, a bargain.

The five hundred colored lithographs were done by J. T. Bowen of Philadelphia. It is believed that the original plates were reduced by means of camera lucida copies from the folio. The octavo edition contains sixty-five additional plates and incorporates the text which had been published separately from the folio. *The Birds of America* achieved immediate popularity and promoted interest in bird-watching for generations to come.

14. **JOHN JAMES AUDUBON and JOHN BACHMAN**
The Quadrupeds of North America.
New York: V. G. Audubon, 1851–54. 3 vols. in parts.

Between 1845 and 1848 Audubon, in collaboration with John Bachman, completed his last major work, the folio edition of the *Quadrupeds of North America*. Audubon's son, John W. Audubon, drew approximately half of the illustrations. The "miniature edition" of the *Quadrupeds* was issued by another son in thirty-one parts at one dollar each after Audubon's death. J. T. Bowen lithographed 155 plates for inclusion in this edition. This set is in the original wrappers.

15. **JANE AUSTEN**
Emma, a Novel.
London: John Murray, 1816. 3 vols.

The fourth and last of the novels published during Jane Austen's lifetime, *Emma* was begun 21 January 1814 and finished 29 March 1815. It was dedicated with permission to the Prince Regent (later George IV), and, though dated 1816, appeared in late December 1815. No writer ever understood better the limits of her own powers; she speaks of "the little bit (two inches wide) of ivory on which I work with so fine a brush . . . " Her novels' charm and delicate humor have won the admiration of innumerable readers. This copy is complete with half titles.

16. **SIR FRANCIS BACON**
The Twoo Bookes of Francis Bacon: Of the Proficience and Aduancement of Learning, Diuine and Humane.
London: Henrie Tomes, 1605.

Bacon was herald of the "new philosophy" (modern science) at the transition between medieval and modern thought. The *Advancement of Learning*, unlike most of his other philosophical works, appeared in English and not in Latin. After disposing of the various objections to learning and enumerating its advantages, Bacon considers various methods of advancing knowledge and the defects of the current practice. It was Bacon's ambition to create a new system of philosophy, based on a right interpretation of nature, to replace that of Aristotle. This copy is bound in gold-stamped vellum.

17. **SIR FRANCIS BACON**
Of the Advancement and Proficience of Learning.
Oxford: Rob. Young & Ed. Forrest, 1640.

First published in Latin (*De augmentis scientiarum*) in 1623, this is an expansion of the *Advancement of Learning* (1605) . It contains a handsome engraved frontispiece portrait of Bacon, who died in 1626, and an engraved title page, both by William Marshall. This copy is of the second issue, and is a large-paper copy in a handsome contemporary stamped binding.

18. **[CHARLES CALVERT, LORD BALTIMORE]**
Articles of Agreement, &c.
[London, 1734?]

The boundary dispute between Lord Baltimore, Proprietor of Maryland, and the Penns, Proprietors of Pennsylvania, was of long standing. In 1732 the parties agreed to carry out a survey, and Benjamin Franklin printed the *Articles of Agreement* in 1733. Here the *Articles* are reprinted and the "Return or Report of the Commissioners" of 24 November 1733 is printed for the first time. The dispute was not finally settled, however, until the Mason-Dixon survey of 1763–67. The document is accompanied by an engraved untitled map which was originally drawn to accompany the manuscript Articles of 1732.

19. **SIR JAMES M. BARRIE**
When a Man's Single: A Tale of Literary Life.
London: Hodder and Stoughton, 1888.

Born in Kirriemuir, near Dundee, and educated at Dumfries and Edinburgh, Barrie was in his early days a journalist. Kirriemuir was reflected in his first two books of sketches, and later and most notably in *A Window in Thrums*. But in this, his third book and first novel, he draws on his journalistic experience, particularly in Nottingham.

20. **[JOHN BARTLETT]**
A Collection of Familiar Quotations.
Cambridge [Mass.]: John Bartlett, 1855.

In 1836, at the age of sixteen, Bartlett was employed in a bookshop in Cambridge, where he became a book lover and student. The shop became a literary haunt for Harvard students and dons, and "Ask John Bartlett" was the customary advice when anyone had difficulty in finding a book or a quotation. Drawn from his commonplace book, the *Familiar Quotations* went through nine editions in his lifetime (he died in 1905) ; it is still a standard reference book. This is a particularly fine copy in the original cloth of the first edition, which, like all reference books, was generally used until it fell apart.

21. **WILLIAM BEAUMONT**
Experiments and Observations on the Gastric Juice, and the Physiology of Digestion.
Plattsburgh: F. P. Allen, 1833.

On 6 June 1822 Alexis St. Martin, a French-Canadian youth, was accidentally shot in the stomach at Mackinac Island. Dr. Beaumont, called to attend him, constructed a flap of tissue to cover the wound which could be raised for observation, so that for the first time the processes of human digestion could be seen. St. Martin ran away in 1825, but Beaumont found him and continued his studies, the results of which were published in 1833. The paper was poor; the illustrations were crude; the typographical errors were many; but the contents constituted the most important contribution ever made to the knowledge of gastric digestion. This is a particularly fine copy in the original boards.

22. **LEWIS C. BECK**
A Gazetteer of the States of Illinois and Missouri.
Albany: Charles R. and George Webster, 1823.

After receiving his medical degree in New York in 1818, Lewis Beck traveled to St. Louis with the intention of practicing in that frontier town. Disappointed with the openings available, Beck decided instead to collect information on the new states of Illinois and Missouri for a gazetteer. Between 1819 and 1822 he traveled on horseback throughout the region making notes on the topography, climate, botany, and early settlements. One of the first large-scale maps of the states, twenty-four miles to the inch, accompanies the gazetteer. Beck obtained data for this map from personal observations and from manuscript surveys that were on deposit in St. Louis and Vandalia, Illinois. This is a fine uncut copy in contemporary boards with printed paper label.

23. **EDWARD BELLAMY**
Looking Backward: 2000–1887.
Boston: Ticknor, 1888.

This work was an immediate best seller and became one of America's most famous utopian romances. Bellamy described in this novel how the evils of a capitalistic society could be eradicated by the peaceful conversion to a socialistic state. The popularity of *Looking Backward* inspired the founding of Bellamy clubs and a Nationalistic party. This is the first edition, first state, in the original green cloth.

24. THOMAS BEWICK
Proofs of *Hstory of British Birds*.
[Newcastle, ca. 1797–1804] 2 vols.

A few copies of the first volume of these proofs were made for Bewick by the shop of Solomon Hodgson, who also printed the book. Bewick probably used them to show to prospective buyers, and to demonstrate to pressmen how he wanted them printed. The proofs of the second volume were made by George Barlow, who was brought from London for the purpose by Edward Walker, its printer.

Notes by a former owner state that the two volumes were originally bound in green morocco (they are now in red morocco three-quarter bindings, with cloth sides) ; that they were Bewick's own shop copies; and that Volume II is unique. However, Thomas Hugo's *The Bewick Collector* (1866) lists several proof copies of both volumes, and there is no evidence to support the claim of Bewick's ownership. In any case, the proofs are fine impressions and have considerable interest; there are also pencil captions on the mounts.

25. BIBLE. ENGLISH
The Holy Bible.
Philadelphia: R. Aitken, 1782.

The first American edition of the Bible in English. When the outbreak of war stopped the importation from England of the usual supply of Bibles (the printing of which was regulated by Royal Warrant), Congress directed Robert Aitken, who had first printed the New Testament in 1778, to undertake a printing of the entire Bible. The resolutions are printed following the title page. The venture was not a success financially, and Aitken lost more than £3000. Although usually bound as two volumes, both are here bound together in one thick volume.

26. BIBLE. LATIN
Manuscript on vellum; 503 leaves.
France (?), middle of the 13th century.

Written in double columns in a small gothic miniscule, this handsome manuscript contains seven historiated initials, some 125 decorated initials, and numerous pen-work initials in red and blue. Its distinctive feature is the fine series of animal interlace

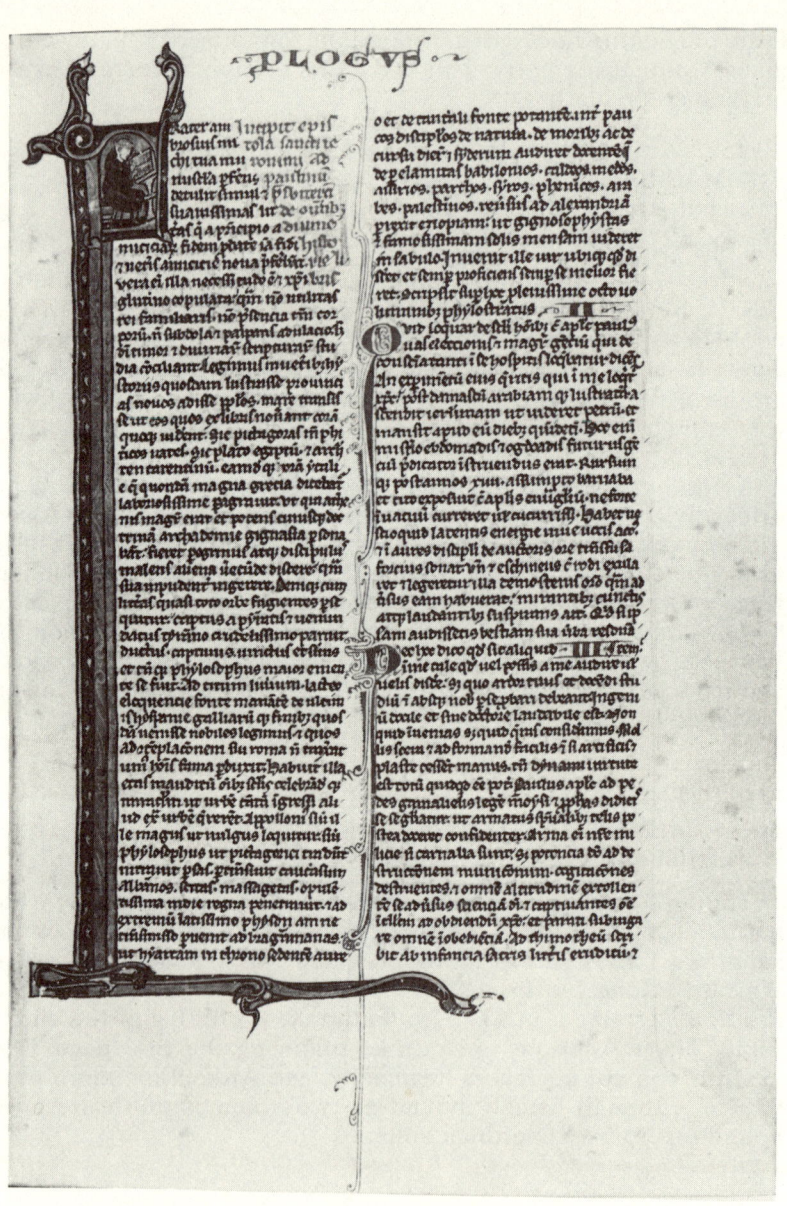

26. Bible (France? mid–13th century)

initials. The artist has displayed great ingenuity in the use of basically similar forms, and no two are exactly alike. Such initials represent a late survival of a style found in Celtic manuscripts of the eighth century. The volume contains bookplates of Fountaine Walker, Laurence W. Hodson, Oliver Henry Perkins, and Cortlandt F. Bishop.

27. **BIBLE. LATIN**
Leaf from the Gutenberg Bible.
[Mainz: Johann Gutenberg, ca. 1450–55]

The Gutenberg Bible was the first book printed with moveable type and the first printed Bible. It has fittingly been called the greatest book in the world. The present leaf, containing the text of Ezekiel 37:11 to 39:7, shows Gutenberg's handsome type and rich black ink (which recent research has shown to be lead and copper, rather than carbon-based) upon white paper, and has been rubricated.

28. **AMBROSE BIERCE**
Tales of Soldiers and Civilians.
San Francisco: E. L. G. Steele, 1891.

Bierce's first newspaper writings appeared in the late 1860's, and in an age of very bitter personal journalism his outspokenness and his caustic wit quickly brought him recognition as "literary dictator" of the Pacific Coast. This, his first volume of short stories, was, in his words, "denied existence by the chief publishing houses of the country" and was published by a merchant friend. The grim and vivid stories, without humor or sentiment, "pointed the way for the American short-story writer."

29. **BLACK HAWK**
Life of Ma-ka-tai-me-she-kia-kiak, or Black Hawk...
Cincinnati, 1833.

Black Hawk, chief of the Sauk and Fox Indians, was a leader in the Black Hawk War of 1832, in which he resisted white settlers on the east side of the Mississippi in Illinois and Wisconsin. Although the militia drove him into Missouri, he returned with his followers to plant corn, and the war began. Many of the starving warriors and their women and children were massacred in Wisconsin by Illinois infantry, but Black Hawk was captured and taken east. His autobiography, written to explain his conduct, was dictated upon his return to Iowa to Antoine Leclaire, interpreter at Fort Armstrong, and prepared for publication by the Rock Island journalist J. B. Patterson. It was many times reprinted, and has become an American classic. This copy is in original boards with cloth back and printed label.

30. **R. D. BLACKMORE**
Lorna Doone: A Romance of Exmoor.
London: Sampson Low, Son, & Marston, 1869. 3 vols.

Blackmore took more pride in his peach trees than in the fourteen novels he produced. Indeed they are mostly forgotten today, apart from *Lorna Doone,* which holds a secure place among English historical novels. Set in the time of Charles II, it is the story of a young Exmoor yeoman whose father has been killed by the Doones, a clan of robbers and murderers inhabiting a neighboring valley on the Devon-Somerset border. Lorna, with whom he falls in love, turns out to be the daughter of a Scottish nobleman. This copy is accompanied by four short autograph letters dated 1895 and 1896 from Blackmore to his American publishers, G. P. Putnam's Sons, about the sale of his portrait.

31. **SIR WILLIAM BLACKSTONE**
Commentaries on the Laws of England.
Oxford: Clarendon Press, 1765–69. 4 vols.

William Blackstone, the most famous of English jurists, studied at Charterhouse and Pembroke College, Oxford. The *Commentaries* provided the first comprehensive description of English law and the constitution as a simple organic structure. Although criticized by Jeremy Bentham and others, Blackstone's work became the authoritative guide to English law.

32. **SIR WILLIAM BLACKSTONE**
Commentaries of the Laws of England.
Philadelphia: Robert Bell, 1771–72. 4 vols.

This first American edition was "reprinted from the British copy, page for page." The *Commentaries* quickly became the principal source on English law for the colonies and the young Republic. A distinguished list of approximately one thousand subscribers appears at the beginning of volume four; each set cost three pounds. The publisher states in his preface, "To the American World," that the publication of the *Commentaries* "will render an essential service to the community, by encouraging native manufactures." This copy is in full contemporary leather.

33. **WILLIAM BLIGH**
A Narrative of the Mutiny, on Board His Majesty's Ship BOUNTY...
London: George Nicol, 1790.

The "Mutiny on the Bounty" with Captain Bligh and Fletcher Christian has passed, through numerous retellings and motion pictures, out of history into folklore; it has the classic ingredients of romantic places, hero and villain, and high adventure. The respective merits of Captain and Officer have been—and will be—long debated. What is not at issue is Bligh's navigational skill, which enabled him to travel 3,600 miles in an open boat and to survive. His account of the mutiny and of his voyage is illustrated with maps and diagrams; this is a very fine uncut copy in the original boards.

34. *The Boston Chronicle.*
Boston: Mein and Fleeming, 28 December 1767–26 December 1768.

Begun as a weekly newspaper on 21 December 1767 by John Mein and John Fleeming, the *Boston Chronicle* was unusual in having been paged consecutively and issued in bound volumes with title pages (not present in this copy). It was also unusual in that Volume I contained an index of six pages (this copy lacks the third leaf). At first the paper included the news of the day, extracts from European publications, John Dickinson's letters of a "Pennsylvania Farmer," and some original essays. Later it became an organ of the Tories, supporting the measures of the British administrators against the colonies, and soon found itself in disfavor. The last issue appeared 25 June 1770.

America's first significant political song, "The Liberty Song; or, In Freedom We're Born," was written by John Dickinson to the English melody "Hearts of Oak." Beginning "Come join hand in hand brave Americans all," it was inspired by the Massachusetts Legislature's "Circular Letter" (11 February 1768) protesting duties and taxes on the colonies. The *Chronicle* of 5 September 1768 printed the words next to an advertisement for the sheet music published by Mein and Fleeming (of which no copy is known to exist).

35. *Boston, December 17, 1773. At the Meeting of the People of Boston, and the Neighbouring Towns at the Old South Meeting House in Boston . . . Occasioned by the Perfidious Acts of Our Restless Enemies . . .*
[Boston: Edes and Gill, 1773]

This broadside gives an account of the final course of events which led to the Boston Tea Party. Several thousand inhabitants from Boston and vicinity gathered on 14 and 16 December in order to avert the unloading of the East India Company's tea. On the afternoon of 16 December, while Francis Rotch tried to obtain clearance for his ship *Dartmouth*, it was voted "that it would be expedient for every town in this province to appoint committees of Inspection to prevent this detested Tea from coming into any of our towns."

BOSTON, December 17, 1773.

At a Meeting of the PEOPLE of Boston, and the neighbouring Towns at the Old South Meeting House in Boston, on Tuesday December 14, 1773, and continued by adjournments to Thursday the 16th of said Month, occasioned by the perfidious Arts of our restless Enemies, to render ineffectual the late Resolutions of the Body of the People.

Mr. SAMUEL PHILLIPS SAVAGE,

A Gentleman of the Town of Weston, was chosen Moderator.

A Motion made and passed that Mr. Rotch Owner of Capt. Hall's ship, be desired to give his attendance.

Captain Bruce, Master of one of the ships with Tea on board, being present, It was moved that he might be asked, Whether he will demand a clearance for his ship of the custom-house, and if refused, enter his Protest, and then proceed on his voyage for London——He replied, that when all his goods were landed, he would demand a clearance, but if refused, he was loth to stand the shot of thirty two pounders.

Mr. Rotch appeared, and was required at his peril to apply immediately to Mr. Collector Harrison for a clearance for his ship; and Benjamin Kent, Esq; with nine other gentlemen, were appointed to proceed with him to the Collector's.

Mr. Rotch returned and acquainted the Body, that he had, accompanied by the above committee, waited on the Collector, and required a clearance for his vessel, as directed; and that the Collector reply'd, that he chose to see the Comptroller first; & at Ten o'clock the next morning he should be ready to give his answer.

It was then moved that this meeting be adjourn'd to Thursday next Ten o'clock, A.M. and that Mr. Rotch and the Committee be desired to wait upon the Collector at the time appointed——And the Meeting was accordingly adjourned.

THURSDAY, December 16. Ten o'Clock, A.M.

Met according to Adjournment

THE Committee to accompany Mr. Rotch to the Collector reported, That Mr. Rotch had made his demand in the following Manner, viz.

"I am required and compell'd at my peril, by a body of people assembled at the old south meeting house, yesterday, where Mr. Samuel Phillips Savage was president, to make a demand of you to give me a clearance for the ship Dartmouth for London in the situation she is now in with the tea on board."

Upon which one of the committee observ'd, that they were present, by order of the body only as witnesses of the before mention'd demand, and the answer that should be given.

Thereupon Mr. Harrison the collector said to Mr. Rotch (Mr. Hallowell the comptroller being present) then it is you make the demand, Mr. Rotch answer'd, yes, and am compell'd at my peril. Then Mr. Harrison said to Mr. Rotch, your ship Dartmouth enter'd with me the 30th November last with dutiable articles on board, for which the duties have not been paid, I cannot therefore give you a clearance until she is discharg'd of those articles, consistent with my duty.

Mr. Rotch attending according to order, was informed, that this Body expect that he will immediately protest against the custom house, and apply to the Governor for his Pass for the Castle, and that his vessel shall this day proceed on her voyage for London.

Mr. Rotch reply'd to this, that he could not comply with their Requirement, because it was impracticable.

Mr. Rotch was then told that he had assured the Body that his Vessel should sail within twenty days of her arrival, which term would this day expire, and being asked whether he would order her to sail this day, he reply'd that he would not.

The Body desired Mr. Rotch to make all possible dispatch in making a protest and procuring a pass for his vessel, and then adjourned till 3 o'-

III o'Clock, P.M. met according to Adjournment.

THE people were informed, that several towns had lately come into measures to prevent the consumption of Tea, whereupon it was mentioned and Voted, that it is the sense of this Body that the use of Tea is improper and pernicious.

Upon a motion made, Voted, That it is the opinion of this Body, that it would be expedient for every town in this province to appoint committees of Inspection to prevent this detested Tea from coming into any of our towns.

It was moved and the question put, Whether it be the sense and determination of this Body to abide by their former Resolutions with respect to the not suffering the Tea to be landed——Which passed in the affirmative. Nem. Con.

It being now half past 4 o'clock, many were desirous and even moved that the meeting should be immediately Dissolved; but some gentlemen of the country informing the Body that their several towns were so very anxious to have full information as to this matter, that they were quite desirous the meeting should be continued untill 6 o'clock, especially as Mr. Rotch had been met with on his way to Milton for a pass, the motion was accordingly over-ruled.

Mr. Rotch returned before 6 o'clock, and informed the Body, that in pursuance of their direction he had waited upon Governor Hutchinson, and demanded of him a pass for his vessel sailing by the Castle, and received for answer, "That he was willing to grant any thing consistent with the laws and his duty to the King, but that he could not give a pass unless the vessel was properly qualified from the Custom-House; but that he should make no distinction between this and any other vessels, provided she was properly cleared ——He further acquainted the Body, that his protest against the Custom House not being finished in season, he could not carry the same with him, but declared, that he had informed the Governor of the steps he had and was taking as to a protest.

Mr. Rotch was then asked, Whether he would send his vessel back with the Tea in her under her present circumstances? who answered that he could not possibly comply, as he apprehended a compliance would prove his ruin.——He was further asked, Whether it was his intention to land the Teas? He reply'd, that he had no business to do in it unless he was called upon by the proper persons, in which case he should attempt to land it for his own security.

The body having manifested an exemplary patience and caution in the methods it had pursued to preserve the Tea, the property of the East India Company, without its being made saleable among us, which must have been fatal to the common-wealth, and to return it safe and untouch'd to its proprietors, and perceiving that in every step they have taken towards this just and salutary purpose, they have been counterworked by the Consignees of the Tea, and their Coadjutors, who have plainly manifested their inclination of throwing the community into the most violent commotions, rather than relinquish and give up the profits of a commission or contract, and the advantages they have imagined from the establishment of an American revenue; and no one being able to point out any thing further that was in the power of this Body to do for the salutary purpose aforesaid——

It was moved and Voted, That this Meeting be immediately dissolved——and it was accordingly dissolved.

---

35. Boston Tea Party broadside, 17 December 1773

Rotch returned to the meeting shortly before six o'clock and informed "the Body that [Governor Hutchinson] was willing to grant any thing consistent with the laws and his duty to the King, but that he could not give a pass" to let the ship go until its tea was unloaded. The meeting was quickly adjourned, the gallery gave a war-whoop, and the crowd hurried to the waterfront to watch the patriots, disguised as Indians, board three vessels and destroy over 90,000 pounds of dutied tea.

As with other important town meetings, an account was immediately printed in broadside form and posted in public places. Printed in double columns, this rare broadside (only one other copy is known) was presumably being set in type while the Sons of Liberty were brewing tea in Boston harbor. This copy is uncut, although a piece has been torn from the bottom left corner with some loss of text.

36. **JAMES BOSWELL**
The Journal of a Tour to the Hebrides with Samuel Johnson.
London: Charles Dilly, 1785.

In 1773 Johnson and Boswell (who had become acquainted in 1763) took their famous tour to the Highlands and the Hebrides. Johnson's account, *A Journey to the Western Islands of Scotland,* was published in 1775, but Boswell's account did not appear until the year after Johnson's death. This is a very fine uncut copy in the original boards, of which Boswell's bibliographer writes, "I have never seen a copy in boards."

37. **NATHANIEL BOWDITCH**
The New American Practical Navigator.
Salem: Cushing & Appleton, 1802.

This work has been called the best book of its kind in the English language. Born in Salem in 1773, Bowditch was a mathematical prodigy who became interested in nautical tables during five seafaring voyages in 1795–1803. On one of them, in 1800, he discovered that there were more than eight thousand errors in J. H. Moore's *The Practical Navigator,* then the primary source for navigational calculation. Bowditch corrected these mistakes and published the first edition of his *New American Practical Navigator* in 1802. His clear and accurate presentation of material guaranteed its success and utility for the young Republic's maritime expansion; the work quickly became the standard aid for ship navigation and went through numerous editions.

38. **SIDNEY BREESE**
Reports of Cases at Common Law and in Chancery Argued and Determined in the Supreme Court of the State of Illinois, from . . . 1819 to the End of . . . 1830.
Kaskaskia: Robert K. Fleming, 1831.

This is the first compilation of Illinois Supreme Court cases, gathered by Breese at the suggestion of members of the Illinois bar. It is dedicated to Elias Kent Kane, with whom Breese read law when he came to Illinois in 1818. Breese financed the publication and even helped set the type. Though the work was not authorized by the legislature, the state subscribed to 150 copies.

39. **CLARE A. BRIGGS**
Oh Skin-nay! The Days of Real Sport [and] *When a Feller Needs a Friend.*
Chicago: P. F. Volland, [1913–14]

Clare Briggs and Wilbur D. Nesbit were both well-known Chicago newspapermen at a time when Chicago journalism was famous. These two books combine verses by Nesbit facing cartoon drawings by Briggs; ostensibly for children, they were bought by adults. These are fine copies of books often found dirty or loose in their bindings.

40. **[WILLIAM HILL BROWN]**
The Power of Sympathy; or, The Triumph of Nature.
Boston: Isaiah Thomas, 1789. 2 vols.

This, the first American novel, although now known to be by Brown, was long attributed to the Boston writer Sarah Wentworth Morton, because it deals with events in her family life: a contemporary scandal of incest and suicide. The frontispiece in Volume I has been called the first imaginative illustration in an American book.

41. **SIR THOMAS BROWNE**
A True and Full Coppy of That Which Was Most Imperfectly and Surreptitiously Printed Before under the Name of RELIGIO MEDICI.
[London]: Andrew Crooke, 1643.

Browne's most famous book was "composed at leisurable hours for his private exercise and satisfaction" about 1635. It has been described as "a confession of Christian faith (qualified by a . . . generally sceptical attitude), and a collection of opinions on a vast number of subjects, more or less connected with religion, expressed with a wealth of fancy and wide erudition." It was first printed

40. William Hill Brown, *The Power of Sympathy* (1789)

without his sanction in 1642, and he therefore determined to issue an authorized edition. It carried his reputation to all parts of Europe in Latin, French, Dutch, and German and has remained a classic. In Rome it was placed on the *Index*.

42. **SIR THOMAS BROWNE**
Hydriotaphia, Urne-Buriall; or, A Discourse of the Sepulchrall Urnes Lately Found in Norfolk. . . .
London: Hen. Brome, 1658.

Browne's point of departure is the discovery of ancient sepulchral urns in Norfolk, which leads him to consider the various modes of disposal of the dead recorded in history and practiced in Britain. The tone is meditative and mystical, and the style reaches the highest level of rhetorical prose. This copy contains at the end the rare leaf with the longitudinal label "Dr. Brown's Garden at Cyrus."

43. **WILLIAM CULLEN BRYANT**
Poems.
Cambridge: Hilliard and Metcalf, 1821.

Bryant's first book of poetry was edited for publication by Richard Henry Dana, Sr., and E. T. Channing. It contains "Thanatopsis," which Bryant wrote at age sixteen and which first appeared in the *North American Review* in 1817. For the book publication, Bryant added the first 17 and last 15 lines of the poem which significantly alter its philosophic significance. This copy is uncut and in the original printed boards.

44. **THOMAS BULFINCH**
The Age of Fable; or, Stories of Gods and Heroes.
Boston: Sanborn, Carter, and Bazin, 1855.

Issued the same year as Bartlett's *Familiar Quotations*, "Bulfinch" has had as long a useful life. Before this, literate America's knowledge of classical mythology was largely derived from the very dull classical dictionary of Professor Charles Anthon. Bulfinch covers the whole field, combining accuracy with charm. This copy is of the first state and is inscribed "Rev. Bennet Tyler, D.D., with the respects of the author." Tyler, formerly president of Dartmouth, then occupied the presidency of the Theological Institute of Connecticut.

45. EDMUND BURKE
The Speech of Edmund Burke, Esq; on Moving His Resolutions for Conciliation with the Colonies, March 22, 1775.
London: J. Dodsley, 1775.

A staunch friend of the American colonies and their interests, Burke here presents his thirteen resolutions for conciliation. His speech took three hours. With the question of the right of taxation he would have nothing to do. "It is not what a lawyer tells me I may do, but what humanity, reason, and justice tell me I ought to do." The resolutions were defeated by 270 to 78. This is a fine uncut copy in the original blue wrappers.

46. EDMUND BURKE
The Speech of Edmund Burke, Esq; on Moving His Resolutions for Conciliation with the Colonies, March 22, 1775.
London: J. Dodsley, 1775.

Another copy in gold-tooled morocco by Mountney.

47. EDMUND BURKE
The Speech of Edmund Burke, Esquire, on Moving His Resolutions for Conciliation with the Colonies, March 22, 1775.
New York: James Rivington, 1775.

The first of many American reprints of Burke's famous speech in behalf of the colonies.

48. EDMUND BURKE
Reflections on the Revolution in France ...
London: J. Dodsley, 1790.

Provoked by a sermon by a non-conformist minister who exulted in the French Revolution and asserted that the English King owes his throne to the choice of the people who can disthrone him, Burke here repudiates this doctrine and shows that nothing was done in the English Revolution of 1689 to give credence to that position. His general conclusion is that the defective instruments of the old regime should have been reformed, not destroyed. The eloquent passage on the downfall of Marie Antoinette leads to the lament that "the age of chivalry is gone."

49. **[REBECCA BURLEND]**
A True Picture of Emigration; or, Fourteen Years in the Interior of North America ...
London: G. Berger, [1848]

In 1831 Mrs. Burlend and her family came from a village near Leeds to Pike County, Illinois, where there were a considerable number of English among the early settlers. The pamphlet is devoted to the trials and experiences of the first few years of the family and is an excellent picture of frontier life: "It is not etiquette in Illinois to sit at the table after you have finished eating; to remain ... implies that you have not had sufficient. This custom I found a very convenient one." The materials and facts were given "viva voce" to her son, who had remained in England, during a brief visit there in 1848; he wrote it up and had it published. This is a very fine copy in the original wrappers.

50. **FRANCES HODGSON BURNETT**
Little Lord Fauntleroy.
New York: Charles Scribner's Sons, 1886.

The first novel by an American—albeit an immigrant from England—to give an extended account, perhaps not wholly accurate, of the "life and culture" of Victorian nobility. "Fauntleroy," says one critic, "was undoubtedly made too perfect ... an insufferable mollycoddle and even a prig. Chiefly he is made up of wardrobe and manners." But despite this fact, he is still an independent American in spirit when he walks unawed into his great inheritance. The story was at once dramatized, and its hero has entered the American imagination. This is a fine copy of the first state.

51. **ROBERT BURNS**
Poems Chiefly in the Scottish Dialect.
Edinburgh: Printed for the author, 1787.

In 1786, in order to obtain funds for a voyage to Jamaica, where a post as a bookkeeper on a plantation had been offered him, Burns published in Kilmarnock the first edition of his early poems. "The epitome of a genius so marvelous and so varied" made him famous, and he moved to Edinburgh instead, where he became noted for his charm and conviviality. The present, second edition of his poems, published in Edinburgh a year later, brought him £500 and enabled him to buy a small farm and to marry one of his many loves. This is a fine uncut copy in the original boards.

52. JONATHAN CARVER
Travels through the Interior Parts of North America in the Years 1766, 1767, and 1768. Third edition.
London: C. Dilly, J. Payne, and J. Phillips, 1781.

At the insistance of Major Robert Rogers, commandant at Mackinac, Carver, a native of Massachusetts, set out for the West in 1766. Traveling through the Great Lakes, Wisconsin, and Minnesota, he finally returned in the fall of 1767 to Mackinac, whence he went to Boston the following spring. The first part of his book is a description of his journey; the second is an account of the manners and customs of the Indians, drawn from other authors. Unable to get his work published, he sailed to England in 1769, where he remained until his death in 1780. The first edition of this often re-issued *Travels* achieved publication in 1778 and brought accusations of plagiarism because of the second part. This third edition, published the year after his death, contains a new index, portrait, and biographical sketch.

53. EVERETT CHAMBERLIN
Chicago and Its Suburbs.
Chicago: T.A. Hungerford, 1874.

Published three years after the Great Fire, Chamberlin's book surveys the history, present condition, and future prospects of Chicago and the surrounding area. It shows the quickness with which Chicago recovered from its disaster and provides a detailed account of the city at the time, as well as such planned suburbs as Frederick Law Olmsted's Riverside and the then-suburbs of Lakeview, Kenwood, Hyde Park, and Woodlawn. It includes numerous illustrations.

54. SAMUEL DE CHAMPLAIN
Les voyages de la Novvelle France occidentale, dicta Canada ...
Paris: Claude Collet, 1632.

The "Father of New France" first sailed for Canada in 1603; Quebec was founded in 1608, and Montreal in 1611. He discovered the lake which bears his name and made voyages as far west as Lake Huron. From 1616 to his death in 1635 he concerned himself with the settlement at Quebec. Accounts of his voyages were published in 1613, 1619, and 1620, but the 1632 edition is the most important. It contains a collective narrative of all preceding French expeditions, as well as Champlain's, and is the only complete edition. This copy, in original calf, has the "Doctrine Chrestienne" in the French and Indian languages and the important large folding map.

55. FRANÇOIS JEAN DE BEAUVOIR,
MARQUIS DE CHASTELLUX
Voyages de M. le Marquis de Chastellux dans l'Amérique Septentrionale . . .
Paris, Prault, 1786. 2 vols.

Chastellux served as a major-general under Rochambeau during the Revolution and traveled extensively from Virginia to New Hampshire in the years 1780–82. His keen observations on both the gay society of wartime Philadelphia and the crude accommodations of backwoods lodging are equally sympathetic and make compulsive reading. This first trustworthy account of life in America at the time of the Revolution was first published unauthorized and incomplete; this is the first authorized and complete edition and includes maps and plates. This copy lacks the half titles.

56. PHILIP DORMER STANHOPE, EARL OF CHESTERFIELD
Letters . . . to His Son, Philip Stanhope, Esq; . . .
London: J. Dodsley, 1774. 2 vols. and supplement.

Lord Chesterfield's famous letters, written to his natural son almost daily from 1737 onwards, were designed for the education of the young man. They are full of sensible instruction, particularly in matters of good breeding, and are admirably expressed. They were published by the son's widow the year after Chesterfield's death. This set has the first volume in the first state and includes the *Supplement to the Letters* issued by the same publisher in 1787.

57. CHICAGO LITERARY CLUB
Club Papers.
Chicago: Chicago Literary Club, 1914–15.

The Chicago Literary Club, founded in 1874, is the oldest literary-social club for men in the city. Members gave (and continue to give) papers at frequent meetings; the publication of selected papers began in 1894 and still continues. This volume contains papers (printed by the Lakeside Press) by Charles B. Reed, Payson S. Wild, and John D. Wild.

58. *Chicago Magazine. The West as It Is. Vol. I, nos. 1–5.*
Chicago: John Gager, 1857.

Published from March through August 1857 for the Chicago Mechanics' Institute, this is the second literary magazine to be published in Chicago, preceded by *The Western Magazine* of 1845–46. It contains literary, historical, and biographical articles, and numerous illustrations, and is a valuable source of information both in the text and in the advertisements. It ceased publication after the fifth number. This set is in the original printed wrappers, as issued.

59. *Chicago Magazine. The West as It Is. Vol. I, nos. 1–5.*
[Chicago: John Gager, 1857]

Another set, bound without the wrappers and advertisements.

60. [SAMUEL LANGHORNE CLEMENS]
The Celebrated Jumping Frog of Calaveras County and Other Sketches, by Mark Twain.
New York: C. H. Webb, 1867.

After going west as a miner and journalist, Mark Twain began his career as a journalistic humorist in the frontier tradition in 1862 in Virginia City, Nevada. "The Celebrated Jumping Frog" first appeared in the New York *Saturday Press* in 1865 and catapulted Twain to fame. As his first book, published when Twain was thirty-two, the present work marks the beginning of one of the greatest writing careers in American literature. This is an immaculate copy of the first printing; it is dated by an early owner June 19, 1867.

61. [SAMUEL LANGHORNE CLEMENS]
The Adventures of Tom Sawyer, by Mark Twain.
Hartford [etc.]: American Publishing Company, 1876.

In this semi-autobiographical story of boyhood, Mark Twain refreshed his spirit from the corruption he had satirized in *The Gilded Age.* The irresponsibility, the love of adventure, and the sense of natural justice presented a sharp contrast to the Sunday School or rags-to-riches literature then standard for children. It has endured for 110 years and is as much a classic today as a century ago. This is a very fine copy of the first printing.

62. [SAMUEL LANGHORNE CLEMENS]
Adventures of Huckleberry Finn (Tom Sawyer's Comrade), by Mark Twain.
New York: Charles L. Webster, 1885.

The sequel to *Tom Sawyer* (1876) was begun the same year but not published until nine years later. While it carries on the picaresque adventures of the characters, it is a more accomplished and a more serious work of art as well as a keener portrayal of regional character and frontier experience. This is a very fine copy, bound in the original black- and gold-stamped green cloth and containing all the earliest bibliographic "points."

63. [SAMUEL LANGHORNE CLEMENS]
Adventures of Huckleberry Finn (Tom Sawyer's Comrade), by Mark Twain.
New York: Charles L. Webster, 1885.

Another copy, in blue cloth. This has the first "points" except for the third state of page 155.

64. **SIR HENRY CLINTON**
Observations on Some Parts of the Answer of Earl Cornwallis to Sir Henry Clinton's Narrative.
London: J. Debrett, 1783.

Commander-in-chief of the British forces in America since 1778, Clinton in 1780 returned to New York and left his second in command, Lord Cornwallis, in the South. After the latter's defeat at Yorktown, Clinton returned to England and published his *Narrative*. His interpretation of events was strongly challenged by Cornwallis; this is Clinton's reply in which he again defends himself.

65. **SIR HENRY CLINTON**
A Letter from Lieut. Gen. Sir Henry Clinton, K.B., to the Commissioners of Public Accounts . . .
London: J. Debrett, 1784.

A further defence of Clinton's conduct of the American Revolution. This is a fine copy stitched as issued.

66. **SIR HENRY CLINTON**
The Narrative of Lieutenant-General Sir Henry Clinton, K.B., Relative to His Conduct . . . in North America . . . Seventh edition.
London: John Debrett, 1785.

With this are bound a copy of Cornwallis's *Answer* (1783) and another copy of Clinton's rejoinder, *Observations* (1783). This volume belonged to Clinton (it bears a family signature "W. H. Clinton") and contains his copious and lengthy manuscript notes in the margins and on inserted leaves. The volume was in the possession of the Clinton family until well into the present century, and the historically important manuscript notes have not yet been studied. Laid in is a small drawing of a house on one of Clinton's American estates.

INTRODUCTION

sapeak, that I knew of then, or indeed that I have heard of since, in which line of battle ships can be received, and protected against a superior naval force: and, as the harbour was the indispensable object, I thought it unnecessary to enter into a description of the disadvantage of the ground, against a land attack, since there remained no other choice.

When the arrival of the French fleet, and the approach of General Washington, were known to Sir Henry Clinton, it will appear by the Correspondence, that his promises of relief in person were uniform; without giving me the smallest particle of discretionary power, different from holding the posts that I occupied. Every reader will therefore be competent to judge, whether, under these circumstances, and as I could not but suppose that the Commander in Chief spoke from a perfect knowledge of his own resources, and of the force of the enemy, it would have been justifiable in me either to abandon, by the evacuation of York, a considerable quantity of artillery, the ships of war, transports, provisions, stores, and hospitals, or, by venturing an action, without the most manifest advantage, to run the risk of precipitating the loss of them.

Although

---

66. Volume of three works (1783–85) containing annotations by Sir Henry Clinton

67. SAMUEL TAYLOR COLERIDGE
Christabel. Kubla Khan: A Vision. The Pains of Sleep.
London: John Murray, 1816.

The first part of "Christabel" and all of "Kubla Khan"—two of Coleridge's finest poems—were written in 1797, and both are fragments of longer works never finished. The moving "Kubla Khan" came to Coleridge in his sleep. After awaking and setting down two or three hundred lines the author was interrupted and, on returning to his task, found the remainder of the poem had passed from memory. But what remains is one of the most famous passages in English poetry.

In "Christabel" Coleridge introduced a new meter and created "one of the most beautiful poems in the English language." This is a fine copy in the original plain wrappers; the advertisements at the end include Jane Austen's *Emma* as "just published."

68. CHRISTOPHER COLLES
A Survey of the Roads of the United States of America.
[New York], 1789.

After arriving in America from Ireland in 1771, Colles spent the next three decades engaged in experimental projects such as proposing a water-supply system for New York, building the first American steam engine, advocating a canal link between the Hudson River and Lake Ontario (prefiguring the Erie Canal), and developing the semaphoric telegraph. But he was ahead of his time, and all his visionary projects for the benefit of the new nation came to naught. "Had I been born a hatter," he said, "men would have come into the world without heads."

No more successful was his *Survey of Roads,* the first American road atlas. It stands today as one of the most valuable detailed historical records of the United States at the time of its creation. Although acquired by several political and scientific leaders, including Washington and Jefferson, it was another failure. This is one of about fourteen complete copies with all the maps issued, the unbound plates being preserved in a contemporary folder inscribed "Sam. B. Webb, 1790." Pasted to the folder is the original *Proposals* for publication (here in its first state); on it is an apparently contemporary price of eight guineas.

69. *The Columbian Magazine for September, 1787.*
Philadelphia: Seddon, Spotswood, Cist, and Trenchard, 1787.

Following "An Historical Account of George of Cappadocia, the Champion of England," and preceding "Love and Constancy: An Anecdote," is the first printing of the U.S. Constitution in a magazine, published the same month the Convention approved it.

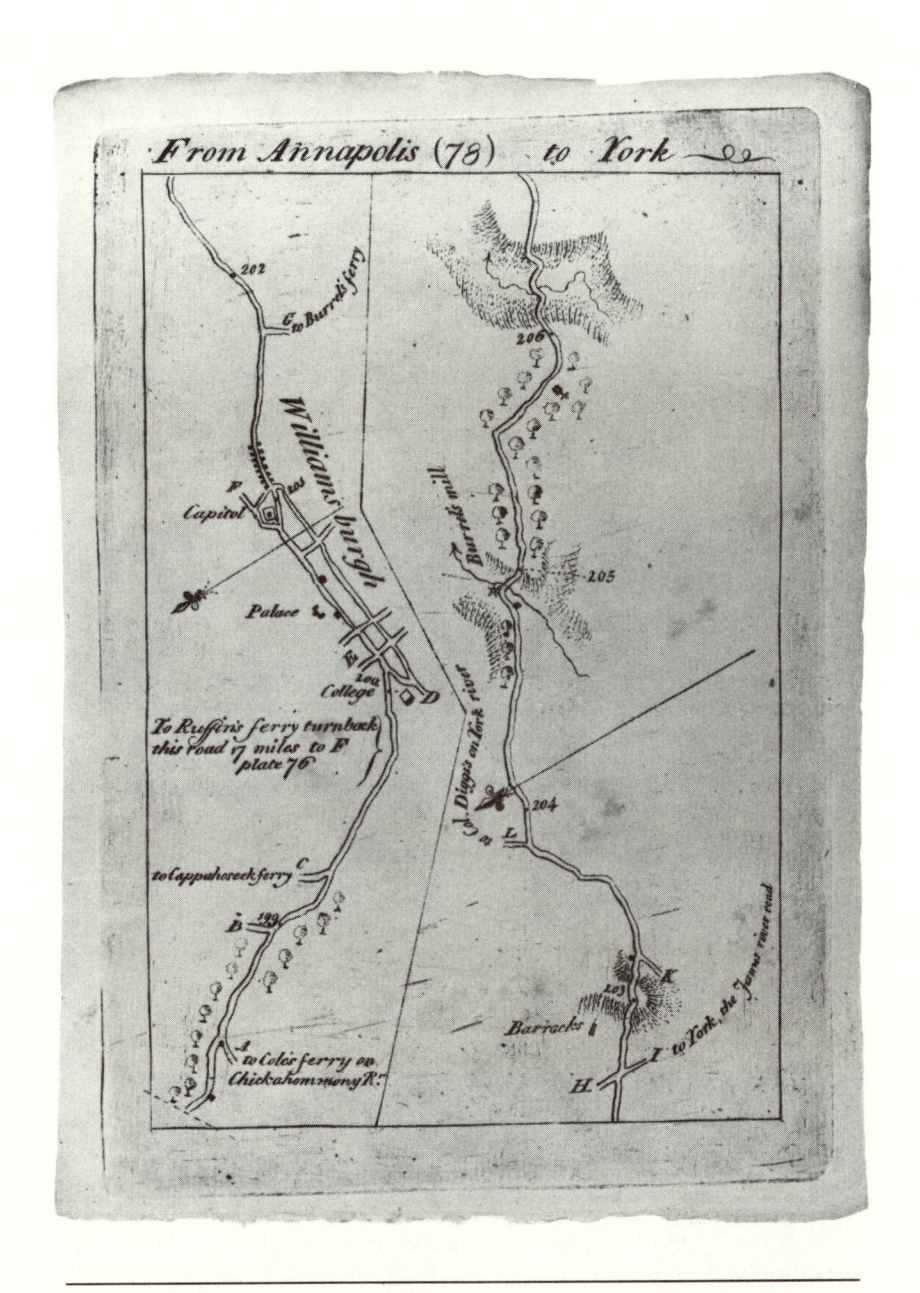

68. Christopher Colles, *A Survey of the Roads of the United States of America* (1789)

Appearing on pages 659–65, it is headed, "The New Plan for a Federal Government." The *Columbian Magazine* was the best magazine of the period, as well as the handsomest, and had some 1,500 subscribers, a large circulation for that time.

70. *The Constitutions of the Several Independent States of America* . . .
Philadelphia: Francis Bailey, 1781.

During the late 1770's the states produced constitutions which typically established a frame of government and specified the powers that the state governments could exercise. This is the first collected edition, "published by order of Congress," of which two hundred copies were printed. Included in the work are the Declaration of Independence, the Articles of Confederation, and two treaties with France. This copy is in a contemporary leather binding.

71. *The Constitutions of the Several Independent States of America* . . .
Philadelphia: Francis Bailey, 1781.

Another copy, also in a contemporary binding.

72. *Constitutions des treize Etats-Unis de l'Amérique.*
Paris: Ph.-D. Pierres, 1783.

Benjamin Franklin had the thirteen state constitutions translated into French by the Duc de la Rochefoucauld, with annotations by Franklin himself. In 1783 Franklin had these translations, along with translations of the Declaration of Independence, the Articles of Confederation, and three major American treaties, printed in Paris by Pierres, the last Royal Printer.
Franklin stated his reason for publishing this work: "The extravagant Misrepresentations of our Political State in foreign Countries, made it appear necessary to give them better information, which I thought could not be more effectually and authentically done, than by publishing a Translation into French . . . " The work has the further distinction of bearing on its title page the first appearance in a book of the Great Seal of the United States. This copy is uncut.

73. *Constitutions des treize Etats-Unis de l'Amérique.*
Paris: Ph.-D. Pierres, 1783.

Another copy, on thick paper (the sheets bulk 5 cm.) in original wrappers and partially unopened. Copies in original wrappers are very scarce, since most of the four hundred issued were immediately bound.

74. *Constitutions des treize Etats-Unis de l'Amérique.*
Paris: Ph.-D. Pierres, 1783.

In addition to the octavo copies, Franklin had a large-paper issue of one hundred copies published in quarto for distribution to all the foreign ministers at Paris for presentation to their heads of government. Most of these copies were printed on Annonay paper, but Franklin had a few, including this copy, printed on *papier-vélin.* (It is thought that Franklin introduced Baskerville's wove paper, the *vélin,* to France in 1777.) On 10 June 1783 Franklin wrote Pierres: "I desire also six of the quarto copies bound in morocco." This is one of those six copies, in a typical and handsome morocco binding of the period.

75. [JAMES FENIMORE COOPER]
The Last of the Mohicans.
Philadelphia: H. C. Carey and I. Lea, 1826. 2 vols.

Cooper's Leather-Stocking Tales, published between 1823 and 1841, established Cooper as an authentic and genuinely American novelist, using native American scenes and situations and developing the "noble savage" image of the Indians. In *The Last of the Mohicans,* the second and best known of the series, Cooper takes the hero (whose name changes from book to book) back to the deeds of his prime, during the French and Indian War. This is an uncut set in the original boards with paper labels.

76. **CHARLES, LORD CORNWALLIS**
An Answer to That Part of the Narrative of Lieutenant-General Sir Henry Clinton, K. B., Which Relates to the Conduct of Lieutenant-General Earl Cornwallis during the Campaign in North America in the Year 1781.
London: J. Debrett, 1783.

Angered by many statements about him in Clinton's *Narrative* about the conduct of the American campaign, Cornwallis wrote this lengthy (260 pages) defense, which started a small flurry of replies and counter-replies. This is an uncut copy in original wrappers and contains two leaves of advertisements and the errata slip. On the title page is the signature "F. Cornwallis," presumably a relative.

74. *Constitutions des treize Etats-Unis de l'Amérique* (1783)

77. **WILLIAM COWPER**
Poems.
London: J. Johnson, 1782. 2 vols.

The first eight pieces in this volume are satires written in the winter of 1780–81 at the suggestion of Mrs. Mary Unwin, with whom Cowper lived. Both John Newton, Cowper's friend and spiritual advisor, and Joseph Johnson, his publisher, made suggestions, which Cowper accepted. Johnson added other recently composed poems, and the book was published in February 1782; it evoked a warm letter of praise from Benjamin Franklin.

78. **WILLIAM COWPER**
The Task.
London: J. Johnson, 1785.

In 1783 Lady Austen, a friend of Cowper's, urged him to try blank verse and, upon his saying he had no subject, told him to write about the sofa in the room. The six books of the poem begin with a mock-Miltonic narrative of the evolution of the sofa, but the author soon turns to himself and his delight in rural scenes and gardening, and his dislike of life in the city. A prefatory note explains the genesis of the poem.

79. **[STEPHEN CRANE]**
Maggie, a Girl of the Streets (A Story of New York), by Johnston Smith.
[New York, 1893]

Written when Crane was twenty-one, *Maggie*, Crane's first book, was far too grim for the magazines, and he published it pseudonymously with $700 borrowed from a brother. Crane was unable to market it, and it sat in his room unsold. Although two small caches later came to light, it has become a legendary modern rarity as well as a modern classic. His success with *The Red Badge of Courage* (1895) enabled Crane to reissue *Maggie* in a revised edition under his own name in 1896. This is a fine unopened copy in the original wrappers.

80. **STEPHEN CRANE**
The Red Badge of Courage.
New York: D. Appleton, 1895.

From reading *Battles and Leaders of the Civil War* and absorbing Winslow Homer's drawings in *Harper's*, but from no actual experience, came this realistic picture of war. "Never, in any American story, had war seemed so actually present." It sold

79. Stephen Crane, *Maggie* (1893)

amazingly, and Crane rose to sudden fame. Its intensity and its startling descriptive phrase struck a new note in American prose. This copy is the first state of the first printing.

81. [MICHEL-GUILLAUME JEAN DE CREVECOEUR]
Letters from an American Farmer . . . by J. Hector St. John, a Farmer in Pennsylvania.
London: Thomas Davies and Lockyer Davis, 1782.

Born in France in 1735, Crèvecoeur became a naturalized New York citizen in 1765. In 1769 he settled on a farm in Orange County, and during the next decade wrote the *Letters from an American Farmer* and also became a Loyalist. As a Loyalist, he went to London where in 1781 he sold fifteen of his letters to Thomas Davies for thirty guineas, and the book appeared the following year. The *Letters* form a series of charming and informative essays describing realistically the physical and social conditions of rural life in America at the time. This uncut copy is in its original boards.

82. [MICHEL-GUILLAUME JEAN DE CREVECOEUR]
Lettres d'un cultivateur américain.
Paris: Cuchet, 1784. 2 vols.

Crèvecoeur returned to Paris in 1781 and was persuaded to translate and expand the original essays for a French edition of his work. In 1784 the *Lettres* was published in two volumes. This copy is in contemporary half calf.

83. *Crockett's Free-and-Easy Song Book . . .*
Philadelphia: James Kay, 1839.

The first edition of this song book was published in 1837 and dedicated to Davy Crockett, who had died at the Alamo in 1836; this second edition is enlarged. The first song, "The Alamo; or, The Death of Crockett," eulogizes Crockett's heroic participation in that battle. The binding is gold-stamped red leather depicting a bust of Crockett.

84. LUTHER S. CUSHING
Manual of Parliamentary Practice.
Boston: William J. Reynolds, 1845.

Cushing compiled this book from his experience as clerk of the Massachusetts House of Representatives. As soon as it appeared, "Cushing's *Manual*," as it soon became known, became a guide for the procedure of all organized assemblies. Its sale was extensive, and thousands of copies were sold abroad as well as in the United States. This copy is in the original binding and is inscribed "Charles Sumner, Esquire, from his friend the author." Sumner, the future congressman, this same year shocked Bostonians by his Fourth of July speech decrying the war he had been invited to celebrate.

85. [RICHARD HENRY DANA, JR.]
Two Years before the Mast.
New-York: Harper & Brothers, 1840.

Dana was obliged to leave Harvard after two years because of eye trouble, and he sailed from Boston in August 1834 as an ordinary seaman on the brig *Pilgrim* around the Horn to San Francisco, and back on the *Alert,* arriving home September 1836. One of the first and freshest—because of its plain, factual nature—of American accounts of the sea, the book has an added importance for its description of pre-Gold Rush California. The book was issued in two bindings; this copy is of the first state of "Harpers' Family Library" printed muslin.

86. [RICHARD HENRY DANA, JR.]
Two Years before the Mast.
New-York: Harper & Brothers, 1840.

Another copy in the same binding; tipped in is an autograph letter to an unidentified recipient by Dana, dated "Old State House, Sept. 16, 1842," stating he is enclosing $100 "on account of Dr. Stevens's list[?]."

87. CHARLES DARWIN
On the Origin of Species by Means of Natural Selection . . .
London: John Murray, 1859.

Darwin's famous voyage on the *Beagle* in 1831–36 was the preparation for his life's work. After reading Thomas Malthus's work on population in 1838, he had a theory to work by, but he did not begin to write his great book until 1856. The whole edition of 1,250 copies sold out on the day of publication. This copy, in the original green cloth, is of that first printing, with the unrevised text.

88. *Davy Crockett's Almanack, of Wild Sports of the West, and Life in the Backwoods . . . 1835 [etc.]*
Nashville [etc.]: 1835–1853. 21 issues.

The *Almanacks* were issued irregularly between 1835 and 1856 by several publishers, accounting for their lack of uniformity in style and text. Although no one knows who was responsible for the early production of the *Almanacks,* it is known that about fifty were printed at Nashville, Boston, New York, and Philadelphia. They contain tall tales based on oral tradition and capitalizing on exploits of such popular frontiersmen as Crockett; indeed, they made him a legendary figure. It has been said they "constitute one of the earliest and perhaps the largest of our cycles of myth, and they are part of a lineage that endures to this day in Kentucky, Tennessee, and the Ozark Mountains." Most of the present twenty-one *Almanacks* are stitched in their original wrappers. This set once belonged to Franklin J. Meine and contains one of the only three or four complete sets of the Nashville imprints (1835–41).

89. [THOMAS DE QUINCEY]
Confessions of an English Opium-Eater.
London: Taylor and Hessey, 1822.

At Worcester College, Oxford, in 1804, De Quincey, feeling himself an outcast and suffering from neuralgia, first began taking opium; over the years he increased his daily dosage to the large quantity of 8,000 drops of laudanum. During this time he became friendly with Coleridge and Wordsworth, though estrangement eventually followed. Here he describes the effects of the drug, chiefly in the form of tumultuous dreams, until, alarmed at the prospect of death, he determined to conquer the habit. (He remained an opium-eater, however, the rest of his life, though he did not die until 1859.) The book first appeared in two issues of the *London Magazine* in 1821, where it caused a sensation; its book appearance in the following year by the same publishers established his reputation. This is an uncut copy in original boards with printed spine label.

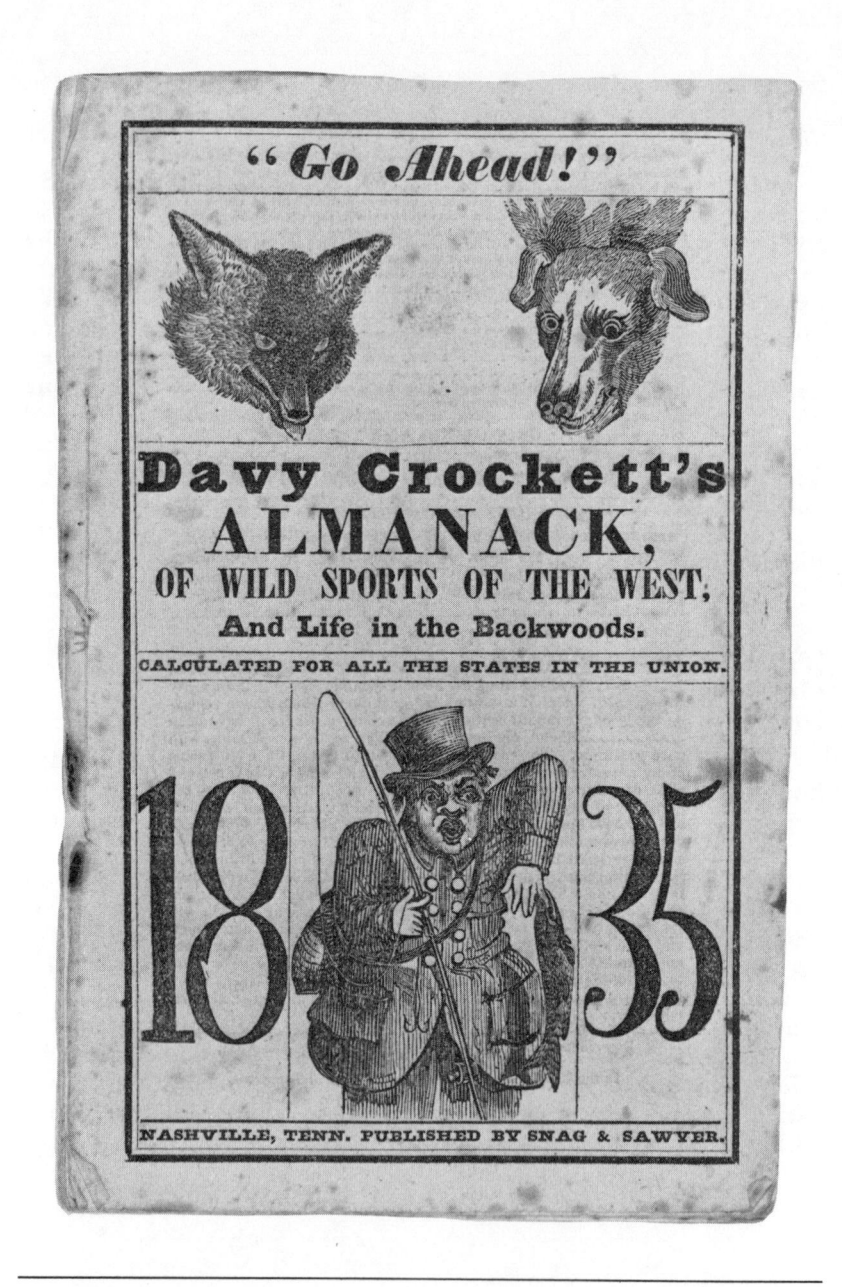

88. The first "Crockett Almanac" (1835)

90. [THOMAS DE QUINCEY]
Confessions of an English Opium-Eater.
London: Taylor and Hessey, 1822.

Another copy, also in the original boards and label, with the final leaf of "Books Published by Taylor and Hessey."

91. [THOMAS DE QUINCEY]
Confessions of an English Opium-Eater, Being an Extract from the Life of a Scholar. First Published in the LONDON MAGAZINE.
Philadelphia: E. Littell; New York: R. Norris Henry, 1823.

This first American edition omits the Appendix and the prefatory matter published in the English edition. This copy is bound in contemporary calf.

92. CHARLES DICKENS
[Christmas Books]
London: Chapman & Hall; Bradbury and Evans, 1844–48. 5 vols.

Annually, from 1843 to 1847 (the books appeared in December of the year preceding the title-page date), Dickens wrote Christmas stories. He described them as "a whimsical sort of masque intended to waken loving and forbearing thoughts," and they greatly added to his popularity. *A Christmas Carol* was the first and remains the most famous; it was followed by *The Chimes, The Cricket on the Hearth, The Battle of Life,* and *The Haunted Man.* Present here are very fine, bright copies of the first issue of each.

93. CHARLES DICKENS
The Mystery of Edwin Drood.
London: Chapman & Hall, 1870.

Dickens began writing his last book in August 1869, and serial publication began in April of the following year. He received the large sum of £7,500 for the book, but died in June before completing it. The solution to the mystery was never disclosed, and an endless number of solutions have been published without really solving the problem. This is a fine set of the six published parts in wrappers, complete with the advertisements as issued.

94. EMILY DICKINSON
Poems [First-Third Series]
Boston: Roberts Brothers, 1890–96. 3 vols.

Emily Dickinson published no book during her lifetime, and only a handful of separate poems appeared in journals. After her death in 1886, her Amherst friend Mabel Loomis Todd, and Thomas

Wentworth Higginson, a poet who had been Dickinson's literary mentor and is now chiefly remembered for encouraging her, published (and somewhat regularized) three selections of her poetry, which was immediately acclaimed. These copies of the first editions are in very fine condition.

95. [CHARLES LUTWIDGE DODGSON]
Alice's Adventures in Wonderland, by Lewis Carroll.
London: Macmillan, 1866.

Dodgson, displeased with the printing of Tenniel's illustrations, had nearly all copies of the first edition of 1865 destroyed, and today it is a legendary rarity. A new edition appeared the following year; this is a copy of the first state in the original binding as fresh as when it was published.

96. **JOHN DOGGETT, JR.**
Doggett's United States Railroad & Ocean Steam Navigation Guide.
New-York: John Doggett, Jr., 1847.

Although England had had its Bradshaw since 1839, this is the first American railway guide. The map (here in its first, uncolored state) shows how few railways there were, and what short distances they ran. The only railway then in Illinois (for which no schedule is given) was the Northern Cross Railway from Springfield to Meredosia on the Illinois River. The map also includes an inset showing the West, which is an accurate map of the pre-Gold Rush period. This is a very fine copy in the original printed wrappers of the first issue, dated September 1847.

97. **STEPHEN A. DOUGLAS**
Kansas, Utah, and the Dred Scott Decision . . .
[Springfield, Illinois? 1857]

Douglas appeared in Springfield on 12 June 1857 at the request of the Grand Jury in attendance on the U.S. Court. In the speech he reiterated his opinions, and those of the Democratic Party in general, on the subjects which were then embroiling the country. Lincoln's speech in reply (a copy of which is in the collection) occurred two weeks later. This copy of Douglas's speech is unstitched and unopened. Only three other copies are recorded.

96. *Doggett's United States Railroad & Ocean Steam Navigation Guide* (1847)

98. **STEPHEN A. DOUGLAS and ABRAHAM LINCOLN**
The Campaign in Illinois: Last Joint Debate ...
Washington: Lemuel Towers, 1858.

In 1858 Lincoln, backed by the new Republican party, undertook to contest the reelection of Senator Douglas. For three months they stumped the state of Illinois and engaged in seven formal debates, all attended by large crowds. The debates had a far-reaching importance and brought Lincoln to national attention. Although Douglas won the election, he was forced to take positions unacceptable to the southern wing of his party, and two years later Lincoln won the presidential election. This last debate at Alton was published in Washington from the account in the *Chicago Daily Times* of 17 October.

99. **DANIEL DRAKE**
A Systematic Treatise ... on the Principal Diseases of the Interior Valley of North America.
Cincinnati: Winthrop B. Smith; Philadelphia: Lippincott, 1850–54. 2 vols.

Drake spent most of his life practicing medicine in Cincinnati. His *Systematic Treatise,* a classic study of disease as related to geography, contains a wealth of information on the topography, population, customs, and diseases of the interior of North America. This is a presentation copy "To Prof. Yandell from his friend Dan Drake." Lunsford Yandell was professor of chemistry and medicine at Louisville Medical Institute.

100. **[HORACE DRESSER]**
The Constable's Guide ...
Binghamton, N.Y.: J. R. Orton, 1832.

Dresser was one of the first lawyers to speak in the courts on behalf of Blacks, and his energies were devoted to defending and assisting fugitive slaves. *The Constable's Guide,* published four years after he graduated from law school, describes the powers and duties of a constable and collector of taxes in New York state. Only two other copies are recorded. This is in its original calf binding.

101. **JOHN DRINKWATER**
Abraham Lincoln: A Play.
Boston: Houghton, Mifflin, [1919]

Drinkwater's popular historical play was first published in London in 1918. For the American edition, two characters' names were changed to make it more historically accurate. This copy of a later printing was inscribed by the author in New York in January 1920.

102. **S. DE WITT DROWN**
Drown's Record and Historical View of Peoria . . .
Peoria: E. O. Woodcock, 1850 [i.e., 1851]

Besides providing a historical account of Peoria, this work contains contemporary information on the town's commercial, civic, and political affairs. Also included are forty-four pages of advertisements as part of the business directory. Drown himself engraved the many maps, charts, plans, and scenes which illustrate the work. According to the author, this was the second bound book to be printed in Peoria. This copy is in original paper-covered boards with cloth backstrip.

103. **MARY BAKER GLOVER (EDDY)**
Science and Health.
Boston: Christian Scientist Publishing Company, 1875.

The publication of *Science and Health* in the autumn of 1875 in an edition of one thousand copies was made possible by two loyal followers who advanced $2,200 for the printing. Only recently had the author gained any disciples, and the Church of Christ, Scientist would not be chartered until 1879. Since then the church has had an influence out of all proportion to its limited membership, and there have been hundreds of editions of the basic document. This is a presentation copy from the publishers to Parker Pillsbury, the advocate of woman suffrage, dated 1877; the errata sheet is pasted in.

104. **JONATHAN EDWARDS**
A Careful and Strict Enquiry into the Modern Prevailing Notions of That Freedom of the Will . . .
Boston: S. Kneeland, 1754.

The profound originality, logical acumen, and critical discrimination in the use of terms entitle Edwards to be called "the first great philosophic intelligence in American history"; the work itself has been called "one of the few great books in English theology." An attack on the Arminian position on free will, it should be remembered with his notorious sermon *Sinners in the Hands of an Angry God* (1741) so that his predestinarianism is not forgotten. His *Enquiry* was widely read in England, and Dr. Johnson told Boswell, "All theory is against the freedom of the will; all experience for it." This copy is of the first issue.

105. **JONATHAN EDWARDS**
A Careful and Strict Enquiry into the Modern Prevailing Notions of That Freedom of the Will . . .
Boston: S. Kneeland, 1754.

This copy is of the second issue; it bears the signature of Mary Hoyte, who is said to have been a member of the Edwards family.

106. **DWIGHT D. EISENHOWER**
Crusade in Europe.
New York: Doubleday, 1948.

The limited edition of Eisenhower's account of the war contains a facsimile of the D-Day proclamation issued to the troops and is signed by the author.

107. **[RALPH WALDO EMERSON]**
Nature.
Boston: James Munroe, 1836.

Based on Emerson's early lectures, *Nature* exhibits the main principles of Transcendentalism. In expressing his belief in the mystical "unity of Nature,—the unity in variety,—which meets us everywhere," Emerson develops his concept of the "Oversoul" or "Universal Mind." Transcendentalism, a reaction against both eighteenth-century rationalism and New England Calvinism, was romantic, idealistic, mystical and individualistic. Its chief exponent, Emerson influenced not only the New England writers of his time, but the entire course of American literature. This copy is of the first state and is inscribed "Caroline Parkman from her husband" (the parents of Francis Parkman, the future historian, two of whose works are in the collection).

108. **[RALPH WALDO EMERSON]**
Nature.
Boston: James Munroe, 1836.

Another copy, this one of the second state and bound by Rivière.

109. **RALPH WALDO EMERSON**
An Oration Delivered before the Phi Beta Kappa Society at Cambridge, August 31, 1837.
Boston: James Munroe, 1837.

This work was later titled "Man Thinking" and still later given the title by which it is known today, "The American Scholar." This clarion cry to think, to create, and to fulfill yourself as an individual, particularly as an *American* individual, burst like a bolt on its audience, on New England, and on the American people, and has stimulated uncounted American youths. This copy is stitched as issued in the original wrappers.

110. **LEWIS EVANS**
Geographical, Historical, Political, Philosophical and Mechanical Essays: The First Containing an Analysis of a General Map of the Middle British Colonies in America and of the Country of the Confederate Indians . . .
Philadelphia: B. Franklin and D. Hall, 1755.

The text urges the settlement of the Ohio country and gives a fascinating account of the sources and methods Evans used in compiling his map. The boundary disputes between France and England over their American possessions caused a large number of maps to be produced representing the interests of each side. Evans forwarded a copy to General Braddock, which he used in the disputed Ohio country, and it is the first map published in America to show that territory. It was the prototype of most of the maps of America for the next half century and was accepted as the standard authority because of the extreme care with which it had been prepared.

111. *Evening Journal—Extra*
Chicago, October 9, 1871.

"The Great Calamity of the Age! Chicago in Ashes!! The Conflagration Still in Progress." Thus proclaims the headline of the extra broadside edition of the *Chicago Evening Journal,* issued approximately sixteen hours after the fire began. "All the principal hotels, all the public buildings, all the banks, all the newspaper offices, all the places of amusement, nearly all the great business edifices, nearly all the railroad depots, the water works, the gas works, several churches, and thousands of private residences and stores have been consumed." The fire razed two-thirds of the city and extended almost to the prairie before rainfall finally brought it to an end late that evening. The *Journal* Office had already burned, and its editors express appreciation "to the Interior Printing Company . . . for accommodations by which we are enabled to issue this Extra." This copy of the first issue, printed in three columns, is mounted on silk.

112. EDWARD EVERETT [and ABRAHAM LINCOLN]
An Oration Delivered on the Battlefield of Gettysburg . . .
New York: Baker & Godwin, 1863.

Everett's long, conventional address and Lincoln's short, brilliant one first appeared in a pamphlet printed in Washington a few days after the occasion. Everett, a famous orator, gave a speech which was at first considered the much more notable of the two. In this New York edition, Lincoln's soon-to-be-classic address appears on the lower half of page 40 in a more accurate text than that printed in Washington. This copy is in the original printed wrappers.

113. *The Farmer's Almanac, Calculated on a New and Improved Plan, for the Year of Our Lord 1793 . . . by Robert B. Thomas.*
Boston: Belknap and Hall, [1792]

Thomas, a self-educated man, edited *The Farmer's Almanac* for over fifty years. From the start the *Almanac* was a success because Thomas knew his audience. Although it sold well in the major coastal cities, the real market (as its title indicates) was in the country, where itinerant peddlers sold thousands of copies to households where an almanac was second in importance only to the Bible. In addition to the farmer's calendar, the *Almanac* contained discussions of events of the day, agricultural advice, court schedules and, of course, select aphorisms—many being of Thomas's own production. The *Almanac* remained in the Thomas family until 1904 and is still published today in New Hampshire as *The Old Farmer's Almanack*. This copy of the first number is stitched and uncut as issued.

114. [*The Federalist*]. Newspaper Clippings.
[New York], 1787–88.

This scrapbook contains the first thirty-three numbers of the original essays. Like many other eighteenth-century contributors, the authors of *The Federalist* chose to write anonymously, and the essays were published in New York newspapers over the signature "Publius." Although the essays were not first published in any single newspaper, numbers one through seventy-seven all made their first appearance in the New York press. Written between October 1787 and March 1788 primarily by Hamilton and Madison (only five were by Jay), the essays were addressed to the people of the state of New York urging the adoption of the federal Constitution, which at that time was before the states for ratification. The inside front cover of this volume is inscribed "33 numbers of the Federalist collected by the Hon. Wm. Cushing." Cushing, a distinguished jurist, was the first associate justice appointed to the

Supreme Court and served as acting Chief Justice during Jay's absence in England; presumably it was he who identified and penned in the authors' names on each essay.

115. *The Federalist.*
New-York: J. and A. McLean, 1788. 2 vols.

The first edition of the eighty-five essays on the Constitution was published in the spring of 1788, Volume I appearing on March 22 with the first thirty-six essays and Volume II on May 28 with the rest. The last eight numbers appeared in Volume II before their publication in newspapers. This edition, corrected by Hamilton, is the source from which most editions of *The Federalist* have been taken. As a commentary on the Constitution, *The Federalist* papers, the most influential American political work, have furnished the principles to guide the Supreme Court in the interpretation of the Constitution itself. This copy is in original boards and uncut.

116. *The Federalist.*
New-York: J. and A. McLean, 1788. 2 vols.

This copy once belonged to Thomas Jefferson and has the characteristic ownership marks "T" and "J" added in both volumes on pages 97 and 217 respectively. On the front flyleaf of Volume I Jefferson noted which numbers were written by Hamilton, Madison, and Jay (in Volume II only Madison's numbers are indicated). The attributions are the same as in Jefferson's large-paper copy now in the Library of Congress; he named Madison as the author of most of the fifteen numbers whose authorship is currently in dispute. In Volume I two newspaper clippings are pasted in (the first a letter from Madison to Thomas Randolph about the Constitution); and in Volume II is pinned a newspaper clipping from the New York *Daily Advertiser* (12 June 1789) describing the proceedings in the House of Representatives concerning Madison's proposed amendments to the Bill of Rights on the previous day.

Andrew Bigelow purchased this copy "in Washington M'ch 1829 at the sale of Mr. Jefferson's Library. The memos on the opposite leaf are in Mr. J's hand writing. Also, the extracts from Newspapers were pasted on by him . . . "; he also owned the copy of the sale catalogue which is in the collection. Bigelow (1795–1877), later a Unitarian minister in Taunton and Boston, was serving the Unitarian Church in Washington for one year. A later pencil signature "Lawrence" is that of William Lawrence (1850–1941), Episcopal Bishop of Massachusetts.

N.° 2.3.4.5.64. by mr Jay.
N.° 10.14.17.18.19. 21.37.38.39.40.41.42.43.
44.45.46.47.48.49.50.51.52.53.54.55.56.57.58.
62.63. by mr Madison.
The rest by Col.° Hamilton

LOUISA, January 13, 1789.

DEAR SIR,

BEING informed, that report has ascribed to me many opinions relating to the public trust, for which I am a Candidate in this District, and being unable to rectify the mistakes by personal explanations, I have thought it proper to give written communications of my real opinions, to several of my acquaintances in your, and the other Counties. It has been with reluctance in every instance, that I have taken such a liberty; and in none have I felt more, than in troubling you with the grounds, on which my services are offered. Whatever hopes I may indulge, that my opinions are not materially inconsonant to yours, and that my pretensions, may not in other respects, be disapproved by you, I have no particular warrant for either, that renders an apology unnecessary. The best, perhaps, I can make, is the one which departs least from the truth; that as far as my opinions, and pretensions, may not receive your approbation, I rely on your candor, for a proper interpretation of the motives, with which they are communicated; and that, as far as I may be favored in both respects, with your approbation, you will not only excuse the liberty I take, but feel sufficient inducements, as opportunities may fall in your way, to set the misinformed part of your county right.

The report, which, I have reason to believe is most injurious, charges me, with being a strenuous advocate for the perfection of the Constitution as it stands, and an inflexible opponent to the change of a single letter. The truth, on the contrary is, that I have ever

116. *The Federalist* (1788). Jefferson's copy.

117. *The Federalist.* Volume II.
New-York: J. and A. McLean, 1788.

   This copy of Volume II is inscribed on the title page, "The Gift of Alex Hamilton Esqr. to Jos. Strong." Joseph Strong, an Albany lawyer, was a clerk in Hamilton's law office from 1786 to 1789.

118. *The Federalist.*
New-York: J. and A. McLean, 1788. 2 vols.

   Another copy, on thick paper; formerly in the collection of Jean Hersholt.

119. *Fergus Historical Series.*
Chicago: Fergus Printing Company, 1876–1903. 35 vols.

   This series recording the early history of Chicago and Illinois was begun in 1876 by Robert Fergus, one of the city's first printers. By the time of his death in 1897, thirty-four numbers had been issued at irregular intervals; number thirty-five was published in 1903. Used judiciously, the Fergus Historical Series provides a wealth of information on Chicago's commercial and social development in the mid-nineteenth century. This is a complete set in original paper wrappers and includes the rare number ten.

120. **HENRY FIELDING**
The History of the Adventures of Joseph Andrews and His Friend Mr. Abraham Adams.
London: A. Millar, 1742. 2 vols.

   The publication of Samuel Richardson's *Pamela* in 1740 provoked Fielding to parody it in *Joseph Andrews* from the point of view of both literary art and morality. Along with Richardson, Fielding enormously influenced the form of the English novel. This set contains bookplates reading "the Right Honble. Charles, Earle of Traquair, 1708" and is stamped on the cover "Traquair House"; the house, on the Tweed, dates from the tenth century and is the oldest inhabited house in Scotland. This set is a fine large copy of the first edition in original calf.

121. **LUTHER FITCH and EDWARD FITCH**
Correspondence.
Portland and Chicago, 1852–56. 76 pieces.

   This correspondence between a young man and his aging father is both amusing and illuminating. The majority of the letters (39 A.L.S. by Edward and 32 retained drafts by his father, Luther) are in two series covering the years 1852 and 1856. In the autumn of 1852, Edward, who is seeking his fortune in Chicago, persistently writes his father, a judge in Portland, Maine, for more money and clothing. He even requests $1,000, a large amount in those days, to join the New Land Agency real estate firm (a circular for which is enclosed). The father writes that Edward is too extragavant and that he cannot send more money, yet he continues to do so.

Despite Edward's recurring failures, he remains optimistic about his new home. In November 1852 he writes his brother that there is probably "no City in the United States growing faster or with better prospects for the future than Chicago—therefore I say Come and Come Soon." It is unusual to have both sides of a correspondence of a modest family from this time and place.

122. GILES FLETCHER
Of the Russe Common Wealth; Or Maner of Gouernement by the Russe Emperour . . .
London: Thomas Charde, 1591.

Giles Fletcher, a scholar and poet, was appointed in 1588 ambassador to Muscovy. While there he was treated with great indignity, and shortly after his return to England he recounted his stay in one of the most important works of Elizabethan travel literature. *Of the Russe Common Wealth* created an immediate sensation among the Eastland merchants in England because of its strong criticism of the Russian government. The dedication to Queen Elizabeth shows the book's attitude: "In their manner of gouernment your Highnesse may see both: A true and strange face of a Tyrannical state (most unlike to your own) without true knowledge of God, without written Lawe, without common justice . . . " The work was quickly suppressed at the request of the English Russian Company and not again published—except in part by Hakluyt and Purchas in their famous collections—until the mid-nineteenth century.

123. JOHN FLORIO
Florio His Firste Fruites, Which Yeelde Familiar Speech, Merie Prouerbes, Wittie Sentences, and Golden Sayings.
London: Thomas Woodcocke, [1578]

John Florio, English teacher of Italian, lexicographer, and translator of Montaigne, matriculated at Magdalen College, Oxford, in 1581. While living in London at the end of the sixteenth century, Florio knew all the chief literary men and their patrons. Dedicated to his patron Robert Dudley, Earl of Leicester, this work consists of grammar lessons, forty-four lively dialogues in parallel Italian and English, and "Necessarie Rules, for Englishmen to Learne to Reade, Speake, and Write True Italian."

FLORIO

His firste Fruites:

which yeelde familiar speech, merie Prouerbes, wittie Sentences, and golden sayings.

Also a perfect Induction to the Italian, and English tongues, as in the Table appeareth.

The like heretofore, neuer by any man published.

¶ Imprinted at the three Cranes in the Vintree, by Thomas Dawson, for Thomas Woodcocke.

---

123. John Florio, *Florio His Firste Fruites* (1578)

124. **JOHN FLORIO**
Florios Second Frutes, To Be Gathered of Twelve Trees, of Diuers but Delightsome Tastes to the Tongues of Italians and Englishmen.
London: Thomas Woodcocke, 1591.

Florios Second Frutes also consists mainly of Italian and English dialogues. The second part of the work is Florio's *Giardino di ricreatione*, a collection of 6,150 Italian proverbs arranged alphabetically. The sonnet, "Phaeton to his Friend Florio," which prefaces this edition, has been ingeniously if not quite convincingly ascribed to Shakespeare. This copy is in the original limp vellum.

125. **JOHN FLORIO**
A Worlde of Wordes; or, Most Copious, and Exact Dictionarie in Italian and English.
London: Edw. Blount, 1598.

In 1598 Florio dedicated his great Italian-English dictionary to Roger, Earl of Rutland, Henry, Earl of Southhampton, and Lucy, Countess of Bedford. His address "To the Reader" is signed "Resolute John Florio," an epithet which stuck. The *Worlde of Wordes* contains about 46,000 definitions, many informative, others racy and idiomatic. This copy of the first edition is bound in the original unlettered calf.

126. **BENJAMIN FRANKLIN**
Experiments and Observations on Electricity, Made at Philadelphia in America.
London: E. Cave, 1751.

This work is America's first great contribution to the study of science. Franklin's interest in electricity began in 1746 when Peter Collinson, English naturalist and book agent for the Library Company of Philadelphia, sent him an account of some new electrical experiments with an "electric tube." Franklin soon began experimenting with this fascinating device and reported his findings to Collinson in a series of letters published in London in 1751.
In these *Experiments*, Franklin suggested the nature of electricity as a single fluid, both positive and negative. Others before Franklin had suggested the identity of lightning and electricity, but he proposed a method of testing the theory by erecting an iron rod on a high tower or steeple. This stitched and uncut copy includes the folding plate and final leaf of advertisements.

127. **BENJAMIN FRANKLIN**
Expériences et observations sur l'électricité faites à Philadelphie en Amérique.
Paris: Durand, 1752.

Thomas Dalibard, who translated the first French edition of Franklin's *Experiments,* also successfully performed the lightning-rod experiment described by Franklin on 10 May 1752 at Marley-la-Valle. Later that summer Franklin developed a simpler method, the famous kite experiment, subsequently described in a supplement to the *Experiments* (1753). This uncut copy of the French translation is in the original marbled wrappers with the paper label on the spine.

128. **[BENJAMIN FRANKLIN]**
Poor Richard Improved for the Year 1758.
Philadelphia: B. Franklin and D. Hall, [1757]

The almanac for 1758 is the twenty-sixth and last in the Poor Richard series personally edited by Franklin. The series, begun in 1732, was immediately successful and commonly sold about ten thousand copies. Besides providing a monthly calendar, Franklin gathered together the world's store of proverbs and aphorisms in these almanacs. The preface for 1758, variously named "Father Abraham's Speech" or "The Way to Wealth," is the most widely reprinted of Franklin's writings. This copy is stitched and uncut.

129. **[BENJAMIN FRANKLIN]**
The Examination of Doctor Benjamin Franklin, before an August Assembly, Relating to the Repeal of the Stamp-Act.
[Philadelphia: Hall and Sellers, 1766]

At the passage of the Stamp Act in 1765, Franklin, then in London, was charged with benefiting from the new law because he had sent some stamped papers to be sold by his partner in Philadelphia. However, his reputation was not tarnished for long. During the debates on the repeal of the Stamp Act in February 1766, he was questioned in the House of Commons. His lucid replies to the 174 questions showed that the tax was contrary to custom and administratively impracticable. The *Examination* was published immediately, and the Stamp Act was repealed in March after much upheaval in the colonies. This is the first American edition.

130. **BENJAMIN FRANKLIN**
Memoires de la vie privée de Benjamin Franklin.
Paris: Buisson, 1791.

Franklin wrote his one book, the *Autobiography,* during three periods in his life between the years 1771 and 1788, carrying the narrative down to 1759. His original intent was to enlighten his son; only later did it become the most widely read of all American autobiographies. The French publisher, Buisson, obtained a draft of the first part of the *Autobiography* (1706–31) and in 1791 the first edition of this work appeared. Various editions and translations subsequently were issued, but the complete work was not published until 1868. For many, Franklin's celebrated *Autobiography* holds the essence of the American way of life.

131. **BENJAMIN FRANKLIN**
Memories de la vie privée de Benjamin Franklin.
Paris: Buisson, 1791.

Another copy, in original wrappers, uncut, with the paper label intact.

132. **BENJAMIN FRANKLIN**
The Private Life of the Late Benjamin Franklin, LL.D.
London: J. Parsons, 1793.

The first English edition of Franklin's *Autobiography* for the years 1706–31, in original boards and uncut.

133. **ABRAHAM FRAUNCE**
The Lawiers Logike . . .
London: Thomas Gubbin and T. Newman, 1588.

Fraunce was a lawyer and also a poet of considerable merit; his patron was Sir Philip Sidney until the latter's death in 1586, whereupon Sidney's sister, the Countess of Pembroke, assumed the patronage. This book contains a verse dedication to the Earl of Pembroke and quotations from Latin and English poets, but its true significance lies in the generally accepted idea that it is the book from which Shakespeare acquired most of his legal knowledge. This is a large copy complete with the folding table.

134. **JOHN CHARLES FREMONT**
Report of the Exploring Expedition to the Rocky Mountains in the Year 1842 and to Oregon and North California in the Years 1843–'44.
Washington: Gales and Seaton, 1845.

Frémont's father-in-law, Senator Thomas Hart Benton, instilled in him the dream of annexing the far West to the United States. He explored, with great endurance, energy, and resourcefulness, the Rockies, the Oregon Trail, and California; in the latter in 1844 he formed a clear impression of Mexico's feeble hold, and his report was a sensation in expansionist Washington, where the Senate ordered 10,000 copies printed. This copy of the *Report* is stabbed and uncut as issued. The accompanying map records much that was new (and does not attempt to show areas unknown to Frémont) and had a powerful effect on the routes chosen by the gold seekers four years later. It was used by the explorer Rufus B. Sage for preparing the map accompanying his *Scenes in the Rocky Mountains* (1846); this is Sage's copy and contains his annotations.

135. **ERNEST FRIGNET and EDMOND CARREY**
Etats-Unis d'Amerique: Les états du North-west et Chicago.
Paris: Jouaust, 1871.

The author gives short descriptions of the midwest states and a longer section on Chicago in this work published just before the Chicago Fire of October 1871. It contains ten important original photographs of the city, including hotels, houses, railroad yards, and general views, mostly in and of the area soon to be destroyed. This copy is in its original printed wrappers, uncut.

136. *Gazette of the United States.*
New-York: John Fenno, 22 August and 23 September 1789.

In ratifying the Constitution, five states requested that a Bill of Rights be added to it. Like many of the state bills of rights, the amendments were closely modeled on the Virginia Declaration of Rights (1776) and included provisions suggested by the Virginia Convention of 1788. During the summer months of 1789, the *Gazette,* a short-lived New York newspaper, published the House and Senate debates on the proposed amendments. On 25 September Congress passed twelve proposed amendments to be sent to the states for ratification. Two days prior to their passage, these amendments were printed in the *Gazette.* Ten of the amendments, commonly known as the Bill of Rights, became part of the Constitution on 15 December 1791 when the necessary number of states had ratified them.

137. **EDMOND CHARLES GENET**
Memorial on the Upward Forces of Fluids . . .
Albany: Packard & Van Benthuysen, 1825.

A child prodigy who gained international recognition at the age of twelve for his translations from Swedish into French, and two years later was translating for his father documents of the American Revolution, Genet became the first French minister to the United States in 1793. A friend of Jefferson and other intellectual and rather radical citizens who tended to favor France over Great Britain, his recall to Jacobin France at Washington's request led to his settling in America and becoming a citizen. His last three decades he spent in peaceful retirement at his farm on the Hudson, conducting agricultural studies and scientific experiments. The present work describes his plan for applying steam power to aeronautics and is the first American book on the subject. This is a fine copy in the original printed boards.

138. **FREDERICK GERHARD**
Illinois as It Is . . .
Chicago: Keen and Lee; Philadelphia: Charles Desilver, 1857.

Gerhard traveled through Illinois in the fall of 1855, and his resultant book is based in part on his own observations and in part on information derived by correspondence with residents of the state. It is a convenient and generally reliable collection of information, much of which is not elsewhere readily accessible. It also contains several maps and illustrations. This copy is in the original publisher's cloth.

139. **JOSIAH WILLARD GIBBS**
"On the Equilibrium of Heterogeneous Substances," in *Transactions of the Connecticut Academy of Arts and Sciences,* III (1876–78), 108–248; 343–524.
New Haven: The Academy, 1876–78.

Following studies abroad, Josiah Gibbs returned to Yale in 1871 as a newly appointed professor of mathematical physics; he served in that capacity for the next thirty-two years. His work "On the Equilibrium of Heterogeneous Substances" remains one of the major achievements in theoretical physics. Here, Gibbs approached the problem of formulating the fundamental principles of dynamics and discussed the vapor densities of a number of substances. The volume is accompanied by a pamphlet, *Josiah Willard Gibbs: Exercises in Celebration of the Fiftieth Anniversary of Publication of His Work on Heterogeneous Substances . . .* (New Haven, 1927), and by Volume II (1871–73) of the *Transactions,* which includes two other essays by Gibbs.

140. **JOHN GOWER**
De confessione amantis.
London: Thomas Berthelette, 1554.

A contemporary of Chaucer, Gower wrote works in French, Latin, and English. The *Confessio amantis* is his chief work in English; it consists of 34,000 lines in short couplets telling stories taken from classical and medieval sources, illustrating the seven deadly sins from the point of view of a weary lover. The poem shows the influence of Chaucer, and the language is substantially the same as his. Gower refers to Chaucer in the *Confessio,* and Chaucer dedicated "Troilus and Criseyde" to "moral Gower," thus affixing that well-known epithet upon him. The first printed edition was by Caxton in 1483; this is the third.

141. **GREAT BRITAIN. LAWS**
An Act for the Promoting and Propagating the Gospel of Jesus Christ in New England.
London: Edward Husband, 1649.

This Act, creating the "Corporation for the Propagation of the Gospel among the Indians in New England," was passed by Parliament 27 July 1649. Edward Winslow, former governor of Plymouth Colony, was instrumental in its formation. The Commissioners of the United Colonies of New England were made the Corporation's agents, and several thousand pounds were raised in England and forwarded to them. These efforts led eventually to John Eliot's famed translation of the Bible into the language of the Massachusetts Indians (Cambridge, 1661–63), the first complete Bible printed in North America.

142. **GREAT BRITAIN. LAWS**
The Acts of Parliament Relating to the Building Fifty New-Churches in and about the Cities of London and Westminster . . .
London, 1716.

Although the London city churches had been rebuilt after the Great Fire of 1666, the expanding population of the metropolis necessitated the creation of more parishes and the provision for churches, cemeteries, and clergymen therein. These laws, enacted in the last years of the reign of Queen Anne and the first of George I, supplied the necessary revenue and other provisions for the purpose.

143. **GREAT BRITAIN. LAWS**
Anno Regni Georgii III . . . At the Parliament Begun and Holden at Westminister, the Nineteenth Day of May, Anno Dom. 1761 . . . to the Tenth Day of January, 1765 . . .
London: Mark Baskett, 1765.

The passing of the notorious Stamp Act in 1765, the first direct tax levied by Parliament upon the American colonies without their representation, has been called "the beginning of the end." Immediately the colonies entered into nonimportation agreements which were so successful that the act was repealed the following year. At the same time Parliament asserted its ultimate authority over the colonies, so that the implications of the act remained to fester for ten years. The importance of the act was immediately apparent, and it was reprinted in several of the colonies. Paged 279–310, this is a very fine copy, stitched and uncut as issued, of the first edition; it bears the signatures Samuel Palmer and Thomas Leigh, both dated 1765.

144. **ANNA KATHARINE GREEN**
The Leavenworth Case: A Lawyer's Story.
New York: G. P. Putnam's Sons, 1878.

While Poe invented the modern detective story, Green, one of America's best known detective writers, established the formula and the popularity of this new literary form. In *The Leavenworth Case,* Green created one of the great detectives, Ebenezer Gryce, who continued to locate clues and track down criminals in a series of twenty-two books. This work caught the popular imagination with its suspense, the cleverness of its unraveling, and the clarity with which it was written. This first edition is in the original rust-colored cloth.

145. **JOHN RICHARD GREEN**
A Short History of the English People.
London: Macmillan, 1892–94. 4 vols.

Green's *Short History,* carefully prepared and twice rewritten, was first published in one thick volume in 1874 and presented the subject with a fullness and unity never before attempted. Its object was to lay hold of the great features of social development and show the progress of popular life. The book immediately attracted many readers with its fresh tone, vigorous style, and unabated enthusiasm. This first illustrated edition appeared ten years after the author's death; this set is bound in polished calf by Bickers and Son.

146. **KATE GREENAWAY**
Under the Window: Pictures and Rhymes for Children.
London: George Routledge and Sons, [1879]

Kate Greenaway studied drawing in several schools before she began to establish her reputation in the 1870's as an illustrator and occasional rhymer of children's books. In 1877 Edmund Evans, the printer and publisher, recognized her talent for depicting an enchanted, ideal world. Greenaway's first real success, *Under the Window*, sold nearly 70,000 copies in England. By the 1880's many of her books were published in editions of over 10,000 copies, and they became popular in the United States as well.

Although many tried to imitate her style, Greenaway had no serious rivals. She acquired much fame and fortune in her time, and her work remains popular today. In this collection there are eleven other children's books by her, all in fine condition: *Kate Greenaway's Birthday Book for Children* (1880), *A Day in a Child's Life* (1881), *Mother Goose* (1881), *Little Ann and Other Poems* (1883), *Dame Wiggins of Lee* (1885), *Marigold Garden* (1885), *A Apple Pie* (1886), *The Queen of the Pirate Isle* (1886), *Kate Greenaway's Book of Games* (1889), *The Pied Piper of Hamelin* (1889), and *The Royal Progress of King Pepito* (1889). Included in the collection is a manuscript receipt, dated June 1, 1890, and signed by Kate Greenaway, acknowledging £50 from her publisher, Edmund Evans.

147. **ISAAC D. GUYER**
History of Chicago; Its Commercial and Manufacturing Interests and Industry...
Chicago: Church, Goodman & Cushing, 1862.

The main interest of this book is its description of Chicago's businesses, trades, hotels, and railroads; it gives a good picture of the city as it was in the midst of the Civil War and nine years before the Chicago Fire. There are numerous illustrations and a number of inserted full-page advertisements, some in color, including ones for the Sherman House and for Edward Mendel, Lithographer, Engraver, and Map Publisher.

148. **ELIJAH M. HAINES**
Historical and Statistical Sketches, of Lake County, State of Illinois...
Waukegan: E. G. Howe, 1852.

Lake County was separated from Cook County in 1839; thirteen years later Haines's history appeared. The first Illinois county history, it is divided in two parts, "the first consisting of general observations; the second gives a minute review of each township . . . " In 1850 the tax collected for Shields Township (which now includes Lake Forest and Lake Bluff) was $641.71. The folding frontispiece is a view of Waukegan (originally called Little-Fort) in 1847. This copy is in its original wrappers.

149. **EDWARD EVERETT HALE**
"The Man without a Country," in *The Atlantic Monthly*, XII (December 1863), 665–79.
Boston: Ticknor and Fields, 1863.

Written to inspire patriotism during the Civil War, Hale's story first appeared in the December 1863 issue of the *Atlantic Monthly*. Although entirely fictitious, it has a realism reminiscent of Defoe. It was widely republished and inspired more patriotic fervor than any other writing of the time. Even into the first half of this century there was hardly a school child who had not read it. This copy of the magazine is unopened.

150. **[ALEXANDER HAMILTON]**
A Full Vindication of the Measures of the Congress, from the Calumnies of Their Enemies . . .
New-York: James Rivington, 1774.

While an undergraduate at King's College (now Columbia University), Hamilton wrote his first pamphlet anonymously at the age of seventeen. A reply to the "Westchester Farmer" tracts, a series of pamphlets by the Rev. Dr. Samuel Seabury (later the first Episcopal Bishop) pleading the Loyalist cause, Hamilton's work demonstrated such a grasp of the issues and knowledge of British and American government that it was at first attributed to John Jay.

151. **JOHN HANCOCK**
An Oration Delivered March 5, 1774 . . . To Commemorate the Bloody Tragedy of the Fifth of March, 1770 . . .
Philadelphia: J. Douglas M'Dougall, 1775.

Orations to commemorate the Boston Massacre of 1770 began the following year and kept alive the spirit of resentment and rebellion. Hancock, on the town committee of the General Court and "the idol of the populace," was chosen to deliver that for 1774. It was widely printed; this is the fifth edition.

152. **THOMAS HARDY**
A.L.S. to Mary St. Leger Harrison.
Dorchester, 18 March 1892. 3 pp.

Mrs. Harrison, the daughter of the novelist Charles Kinglsey, was herself a successful novelist under the pseudonym Lucas Malet. In this letter Hardy thanks her for sending "a novel which I am now glad I did not buy": no doubt her *The Wages of Sin,* which was published in 1891 and to which he refers in a letter written on 14 April to a woman suffrage leader. He promises to send the new edition of *Tess of the D'Urbervilles* when it appears and briefly discusses the advantages and disadvantages of women in society. The letter was formerly in the collection of Carroll A. Wilson, in whose catalogue it is partially published.

153. **THOMAS HARRIOT**
Admiranda narratio fida tamen de commodis et incolarum ritibus Virginiae . . .
Frankfort: Theodor de Bry, 1590.

Sir Walter Raleigh sent Harriot as scientific advisor, and John White as artist, on the Roanoke expedition of 1585–86. Harriot's *Brief and True Report* was published in 1588; De Bry combined the work of the two and published the account in Latin, French, and German as the first part of his great "Voyages," whereupon it became one of the principal sources of information about North America and its inhabitants for over a century. White's illustrations are considered the most authentic depiction of American Indians of the time. (Other illustrations by him accompany Le Moyne de Margues's account, which is also in the collection.) This copy, a mixed issue (as are most copies) of the first edition, is bound in gold-stamped morocco by Pratt.

154. **JOEL CHANDLER HARRIS**
Uncle Remus: His Songs and His Sayings.
New York: D. Appleton, 1881.

Harris's first Uncle Remus story appeared in the Atlanta *Constitution* in 1879; this first collection was an instant success and precipitated the greatest flood of dialect literature the country had known. Subtitled "Myths and Legends of the Old Plantation," it contains thirty-four tales in Negro dialect as well as the "songs and sayings." Uncle Remus is both typical and strongly individual, and his tales are told with a simple humor and authentic dialect. This copy is of the first printing.

155. **JOEL CHANDLER HARRIS**
Nights with Uncle Remus.
Boston: James R. Osgood, 1883.

   The second of the Uncle Remus books. This and its predecessor are secure in their place among the unforgettable books in American literature.

156. **JOEL CHANDLER HARRIS**
On the Plantation.
New York: D. Appleton, 1892.

   During the 1890's Harris published thirteen books, a number of them for children. Subtitled "A Story of a Georgia Boy's Adventures during the War," this too is written in dialect and is partly autobiographical.

157. **BRET HARTE**
The Luck of Roaring Camp, and Other Sketches.
Boston: Fields, Osgood, 1870.

   Harte's local-color stories had been appearing for several years in California newspapers and in the *Overland Monthly,* of which he was editor, and he had published two collections. This volume swept him into popular favor throughout the country, and he contracted with the *Atlantic Monthly* for twelve contributions for $10,000. In addition to the title story, the book also contains the well-known "M'Liss" and "Tennessee's Partner."

158. **HARVARD UNIVERSITY**
Order of Services at the Centennial Celebration of Harvard University on the 8th of September, 1836.
[Cambridge? 1836]

   Three years after Chicago was incorporated as a village, Harvard celebrated its bicentennial with great pomp and ceremony. President Quincy's address "commanded, during two hours, the attention of the audience," and the Ode, by the Rev. Samuel Gilman, was sung for the first time. Beginning "Fair Harvard! Thy sons to thy Jubilee throng," it was to become sacred to generations of Harvard men. The words are printed on this program for the first time. (The reporting in the *National Union Catalog* of two other broadsides with similar titles, *Order of Exercises at the Centennial Celebration* and *Order of the Celebration,* is in error; they prove on examination to have the title as given above.)

159. **NATHANIEL HAWTHORNE**
Twice-Told Tales.
Boston: American Stationers Co., 1837.

This is Hawthorne's first published book, preceded only by the privately published and later suppressed *Fanshawe* (1828). Many of the thirty-nine stories in the volume are marked by the author's interest in the supernatural and deal with Puritanism and its effect in New England history. An enlarged edition was published in 1842.

160. **NATHANIEL HAWTHORNE**
Mosses from an Old Manse.
New York: Wiley and Putnam, 1846.

Written while Hawthorne lived in the Old Manse in Concord, these twenty-five short stories and historical sketches continue his exploration and analysis of the Puritan mind. They include such well-known stories as "The Celestial Railroad," "Rappaccini's Daughter," and "The Birthmark." This set of the two parts is in original wrappers.

161. **NATHANIEL HAWTHORNE**
Mosses from an Old Manse.
New York: Wiley and Putnam, 1846.

Another set, also in the original wrappers.

162. **NATHANIEL HAWTHORNE**
The Scarlet Letter.
Boston: Ticknor, Reed, and Fields, 1850.

Hawthorne's greatest book and one of the landmarks of American literature was written after he was dismissed as Surveyor of the Port of Salem because of a change of political administration. It sums up in classic terms the Puritan dilemma that had so long occupied his imagination. This copy has the printed catalogue bound before the flyleaf.

163. **NATHANIEL HAWTHORNE**
The Scarlet Letter.
Boston: Ticknor, Reed, and Fields, 1850.

    Another copy, this with the catalogue (in a variant state) bound after the flyleaf.

164. **NATHANIEL HAWTHORNE**
The House of the Seven Gables.
Boston: Ticknor, Reed, and Fields, 1851.

    Published in the same year as *Moby-Dick* and *Leaves of Grass*, Hawthorne's book is also a classic. It is based on the tradition of a curse pronounced on the author's family when his great-grandfather was a judge in the Salem witchcraft trials. The house was described from an actual house in Salem, and the household depicted was in some respects like that of Hawthorne's youth: withdrawn, solitary, and haunted by an ancestral curse.

165. **ERNEST HEMINGWAY**
Three Stories & Ten Poems.
Paris: Contact Publishing Co., [1923]

    Hemingway's first book was published in an edition of three hundred copies in the fall of 1923, two years after he arrived in Paris, by Robert McAlmon, the American writer and publisher who also lived there. The poems are not notable, but the stories show the beginning of the famous "Hemingway style" of concise, unadorned sentences which would reach maturity in his next two books, *In Our Time* and *The Sun Also Rises*. This is a presentation copy "To the author of Doodab from one of his boyhood friends." *Doodab*, by Harold Loeb, Hemingway's friend and fellow expatriate, was published in 1925.

166. **ERNEST HEMINGWAY**
Today Is Friday.
[Englewood, New Jersey: As Stable Publications, 1926]

    Hemingway's first play has been called "a tasteless little account of the aftermath of the Crucifixion." It was published in an edition of three hundred copies with a drawing by Jean Cocteau, and collected the following year in *Men without Women*. His next play was not written until 1937.

167. **ERNEST HEMINGWAY**
The Old Man and the Sea.
New York: Charles Scribner's Sons, 1952.

A parable of man's struggle with the natural world, this book restored Hemingway's reputation as a major writer. It won him the Pulitzer Prize in 1953 and was instrumental in his winning the Nobel Prize in 1954. It was the last book to be published before his death in 1961.

168. **ERNEST HEMINGWAY**
A Moveable Feast.
New York: Charles Scribner's Sons, 1964.

Subtitled "Sketches of the Author's Life in Paris in the Twenties," the pieces here published were begun in 1957, put aside in 1960 to write *The Dangerous Summer,* and left unpublished at the author's death in 1961. Hemingway's first posthumously published book, it was deservedly popular and had a large sale.

169. **WILLIAM H. HERNDON**
Herndon's Lincoln: The True Story of a Great Life.
Chicago [etc]: Belford, Clarke, 1889. 3 vols.

William Herndon joined Lincoln's law practice in 1844 and became a great admirer. Based on Herndon's first-hand knowledge and later researches, this biography (written by Jesse W. Weik with the text approved by Herndon) has remained the single most authoritative source for Lincoln's early period. Immediately following the assassination, Herndon began to collect reminiscences of Lincoln's childhood and boyhood from men still living. For numerous reasons, the publication of the planned biography was delayed for more than twenty years while others used Herndon's materials for their own biographies. Although this work was severely criticized when it appeared for statements concerning the birth of Lincoln's mother, his religious beliefs, and other details, "yet to him, more than any other writer, we owe our knowledge of Lincoln the man."

170 *Historisch-genealogischer calender; oder, Jahrbuch der markwürdigsten neuen welt begebenheiten für 1784.*
Leipzig: Haude und Spener, [1783]

More than half of this Yearbook is a long account of the American Revolution by Matthias Christian Sprengel, professor of history at the University of Halle, whose earlier version, the first in German, had appeared the previous year. It contains a folding map

170. *Historisch-genealogischer calender* (1783)

of the colonies extending to the Mississippi Valley, eighteen plates (including the Boston Tea Party, the Battles of Lexington and Bunker Hill, Franklin at Versailles, and Cornwallis at Yorktown); three of them are colored and show the American flag (its first appearance in a book) and the most authentic contemporary depictions of American military uniforms. This copy is in its original glazed paper boards.

171 THOMAS HOBBES
Leviathan; or, The Matter, Forme, & Power of a Common-wealth Ecclesiasticall and Civill.
London: Andrew Crooke, 1651.

Thomas Hobbes was born at Malmesbury in 1588 and educated at Magdalen Hall, Oxford. He held that man is fundamentally a selfish creature. In the *Leviathan,* a term symbolizing sovereign power, Hobbes expounded on the political state, outside of which there exists a war of every man against every man and where life is nasty, brutish, and short—a far cry from, but perhaps more realistic than, John Locke's state of nature. The publication of this work brought him into general disfavor on both political and religious grounds. This is a copy of the first edition identified by the "head" ornament on the printed title page.

172. [OLIVER WENDELL HOLMES]
The Autocrat of the Breakfast-Table.
Boston: Phillips, Sampson, 1858.

Born in Cambridge and reared in the traditions of the Brahmin class, Holmes received his medical degree from Harvard in 1836 and later taught anatomy there. He was also an essayist and witty conversationalist and became the unofficial poet laureate of Boston. Beginning with the November 1857 issue of the *Atlantic Monthly,* the *Autocrat* ran for twelve numbers; the book appeared on 12 November 1858 and became the best seller of the day. These rambling Addisonian essays describe imaginary table-talk at a Boston boarding-house, providing a distillation of the intellectual and cultural life of New England at its zenith. This copy is in the rare "five-star" binding.

173. OLIVER WENDELL HOLMES, JR.
The Common Law.
Boston: Little, Brown, 1881.

One of the true world classics in legal literature, *The Common Law* grew out of ten years' thought and scholarship while Holmes taught at Harvard. Holmes saw the law as both a development from the past and an organism of the present to be molded to the changing needs of a society. "The life of the law has not been logic: it has been experience." In 1902 Holmes accepted appointment to the United States Supreme Court where he served for thirty years and became known as "the great dissenter." This copy is in a green cloth binding.

174. OLIVER WENDELL HOLMES, JR.
The Common Law.
Boston: Little, Brown, 1881.

Another copy, in brick cloth binding.

175. L. EMMETT HOLT
The Care and Feeding of Children.
New York: D. Appleton, 1894.

The Babies' Hospital of New York City, the first of its kind, was founded in 1887 and became internationally known under Holt's leadership. In 1894 he published this question-and-answer text to guide mothers in the care and feeding of children. The Dr. Spock of its time, it ran through seventy-five printings, was translated into three languages, and established scientific common sense in the American nursery.

176. [DANIEL HORSMANDEN]
A Journal of the Proceedings in the Detection of the Conspiracy Formed by Some White People, in Conjunction with Negro and Other Slaves, for Burning the City of New-York in America, and Murdering the Inhabitants...
New-York: James Parker, 1744.

This is the first edition of the work now known as Horsmanden's "Negro Plot of 1741," an event which threw New York City into a state of near panic comparable to, if shorter than, the Salem witchcraft episode. Horsmanden, the City Recorder, published the *Proceedings* for several reasons: to justify the extreme actions taken; to urge the citizens to tighten regulation of the black, mostly slave, residents (at that time about one-sixth of the city's total population of 12,000); and to make money.

The several fires were probably the acts of only a few of the 20 whites and 154 blacks indicted. Though no real evidence of a plot was established, two-thirds of the accused were found guilty. From the list at the end of the book we learn their fate: 18 blacks and 2 white persons hanged; 13 blacks burned at the stake; and 70 blacks transported. This copy belonged to the English antiquarian Daniel Wray.

177. **WILLIAM DEAN HOWELLS**
The Rise of Silas Lapham.
Boston: Ticknor, 1885.

   The first novel concerning the self-made American is written with the same deep egalitarianism that characterizes all Howells's work. He made the new realism, and all at once America found that she was full of material for fiction. Every provincial environment produced its recorder, and the novel of locality for a time dominated American literature. Within two weeks of the book's publication, eight thousand copies had been sold; this copy is of the first printing.

178. **[THOMAS HUGHES]**
Tom Brown's School Days, by an Old Boy.
Cambridge: Macmillan, 1857.

   Educated at Rugby and Oriel College, Oxford, Hughes tells the story of an ordinary schoolboy at Rugby under the headmastership of the famous Dr. Thomas Arnold, whose leadership took the school to the first rank. The book depicts schoolboy cruelties and loyalties and had a considerable influence on public schools. It was immediately successful—five editions were issued in nine months—and became the most popular schoolboy tale in the English language. This copy of the first edition is bound in morocco by Zaehnsdorf.

179. **THOMAS HUTCHINS**
A New Map of the Western Parts of Virginia, Pennsylvania, Maryland, and North Carolina . . .
London: T. Hutchins, 1778.

   This map was published at the same time, though separately, as Hutchins's *Topographical Description* of the same areas. The map extends from the Allegheny Mountains on the east to a little west of the Mississippi, and to the mouth of the Arkansas River on the south. Much of it was based on his own explorations while in the military and was by far the best map of the West to that time. Hutchins was imprisoned in England after the Revolution broke out; after returning to America he was appointed Geographer to the United States in 1781 and later surveyed parts of the Northwest Territory.

180. **ALDOUS HUXLEY**
Brave New World.
London: Chatto & Windus, 1932.

Huxley's first books were poetry, but his reputation was established with his witty, cynical novels, beginning with *Chrome Yellow* in 1921. With *Brave New World* he turned his formidable intellect to something in the air which he both feared and detested: a vision of the nightmarish lengths to which psychological conditioning can be taken. All too prophetic, the book has become a classic. This copy is one of 324 on special paper and is signed by the author.

181. **ILLINOIS. CONSTITUTION**
Constitution of the State of Illinois . . . Printed by Order of the House of Representatives.
Washington City: E. De Krafft, 1818.

A constitutional convention held at Kaskaskia in August 1818 resulted in a constitution adopted 26 August. It was printed there (of which edition a half-dozen copies are known) and reprinted in Washington. The Constitution was ratified without a popular vote, and Illinois was admitted to the United States as the twenty-first state on 3 December by resolution of the U.S. Congress. The first governor was former territorial delegate Shadrach Bond, and the capital was Kaskaskia.

182. **ILLINOIS. CONSTITUTION**
The Constitution of the State of Illinois . . .
Chicago: Western News Company, 1870.

The Illinois Constitution of 1848, which replaced that of 1818, proved inadequate in several respects, but a proposed Constitution of 1862 was rejected. A convention called in 1869 produced a Constitution which was ratified 2 July 1870; it made salaries for state officials a matter for legislation (instead of having them fixed), prohibited special legislation on twenty-three subjects, and reorganized the judicial system. This Constitution (with amendments) remained in force a full century.

183. **ILLINOIS. CONSTITUTION**
Constitution of the State of Illinois, 1970.
[Springfield? 1970]

After a century of use, the 1870 Constitution needed revision, and a Constitutional Convention was held from December 1969 to September 1970, resulting in this document, the current Illinois Constitution.

184. *Illustrations of Greater Chicago.*
Chicago: J. M. Wing; New York: A. J. Bicknell, 1875.

Published four years after the Chicago Fire by the publisher of *The Land Owner,* these large illustrations show how far the city had come in remedying the devastation. All types of buildings are shown, including a number of interiors. One of the illustrations shows the factory of E. W. Blatchford, the first president of the board of The Newberry Library; others show the McCormick Reaper Works and the Tribune Building.

185. **GILBERT IMLAY**
A Topographical Description of the Western Territory of North America . . . the Third Edition with Great Additions.
London: J. Debrett, 1797.

After service in the Revolution, Imlay lived in Kentucky from March 1783 to the end of 1785, when he moved permanently abroad. First published in 1792, this is the most complete edition of the best book of its time concerning the territories west of the Allegheny Mountains. It contains a number of accounts reprinted from other sources brought conveniently together. It is also permeated with contemporary European radical thought, an interest in which involved Imlay in an affair (begun in 1793) with Mary Wollstonecraft, author of *The Rights of Woman,* a copy of which is in the collection. (She bore him a daughter and told of his ungenerous conduct in her posthumous *Memoirs.*)

186. **WASHINGTON IRVING**
A History of New York . . . by Diedrich Knickerbocker.
New York [etc.]: Inskeep & Bradford, 1809. 2 vols.

In 1807 Samuel Latham Mitchell published a book on New York so ponderous and pretentious as to be ridiculous. Irving started to write a parody of Mitchell, but instead found himself writing a comic history of old New York, a "sprawling burlesque" in a compound of sense and nonsense which still entertains. Widely published and translated, this has been called the first completely original non-scholarly American book, as well as the first great work of American comic literature. This copy was formerly in the collection of Carroll A. Wilson.

187. **HELEN HUNT JACKSON**
Ramona: A Story.
Boston: Roberts Brothers, 1884.

Born in Amherst, Helen Hunt went west in 1872, married, and made her home there the rest of her life. She took an interest in the Indians and after considerable research wrote *A Century of*

Dishonor in 1881, a devastating indictment which she sent to each member of Congress. In 1882 she was appointed a special commissioner to investigate the conditions of the Mission Indians in California. When she felt her efforts had brought no results, she turned to fiction to set forth her indictment of the treachery and cruelty of the government's treatment of the Indians. *Ramona* was the result, and it had a wide popularity. This is a fine copy of a book which was printed on inferior paper.

188. [JONATHAN JACKSON]
Thoughts upon the Political Situation of the United States of America . . . with Some Observations on the Constitution for a Federal Government . . . by a Native of Boston.
Worcester: Isaiah Thomas, 1788.

The author arrives in a most leisurely manner at his conclusion that the Constitution should be ratified, while he comments, as he goes along, on matters that have nothing to do with the subject at hand. He condemns opulence and drunkenness as unbecoming to a republic, and warns the country to be on guard against European influence in politics and fashion alike.

189. **JOHN JAY**
A.L.S. to Mrs. Margaret Cadwalader Meredith.
Aranjues, Spain, 12 May 1780. 7 pp.

Jay wrote this letter to Mrs. Meredith (wife of Samuel Meredith, a Philadelphia merchant and first Treasurer of the United States) while serving as American Minister to Spain. Lamenting his absence from the American scene, Jay says he longs for the shores of the Hudson and the Delaware where "I shall again have the Pleasure of seeing you shine in the Dance, at the Tea Table, and in those polite and proportioned attentions which bespeak Discernment as well as Grace." He also apologizes for not sending along promised silks and gives a description of the Spanish town.

In the second half of the letter, Jay alludes to the building of a new federal city: "When I return, we will put all our Castles together; and be the founders of a visionary City, that will probably surpass Mr. Penn's real one. My only apprehension is, that Betsey [probably Elizabeth Meredith Clymer] will be for having too many Churches in it." The letter shows Jay's keenness of observation, sense of humor, and graceful style.

190. **JOHN JAY**
Autograph manuscript of Essay No. 3 of *The Federalist.*
New York, 1787. 5 pp.

After serving as one of the peace commissioners to England, Jay was appointed as Secretary of Foreign Affairs for the Continental Congress (1784–89). During his tenure, Jay's power was weakened by the impotence of the Union under the Articles of Confederation, and he became one of the strongest advocates for a new constitution. Jay's five essays (nos. 2, 3, 4, 5, 64) were written in great haste in ten days in the autumn of 1787. His second, published as Essay 3 in the *Independent Journal* on November 3rd, deals with security from foreign hostilities and an analysis of "just" wars. His manuscript draft contains hundreds of revisions and tends to show the tightening of his prose and of his argument. Only three other drafts (nos. 4, 5, 64) from *The Federalist,* all by Jay, are known to have survived.

191. **JOHN JAY**
A.L.S. to John Adams.
Albany, 2 January 1801. 1 p.

In this letter Jay, then Governor of New York, declines the President's renomination as United States Chief Justice, stating political and personal reasons. (Adams's official letter of nomination to Jay is also in the collection, as are John Marshall's letter as Secretary of State to Jay and Jay's response, all on the same subject.) Jay writes, "I left the bench perfectly convinced that under a system so defective it would not obtain the Energy, Weight, and Dignity which are essential to its affording due support to the national government . . . " This situation quickly changed under the leadership of John Marshall. Jay also mentions "the state of my health" as an additional factor in his decision. He retired from public life in 1801 and lived his remaining twenty-eight years on his farm in Bedford, New York.

192. **JOHN JAY**
A.L.S. to John Marshall.
Albany, 2 January 1801. 1 p.

Restating his reasons to Secretary of State John Marshall for declining the office of Chief Justice, Jay promptly returned the official commission. (Marshall's letter is also in the collection.) Upon receiving this news from Jay, President Adams and Secretary Marshall met to discuss who should be the next nominee. Marshall recounted this meeting and his surprise when Adams said, "I believe I must nominate you." Marshall, a staunch Federalist,

190. John Jay, Manuscript of *Federalist* Essay No. 3 (1787)

accepted the nomination and served in this capacity for the next thirty-five years, increasing the power and prestige of the judicial branch of the federal government.

193. [THOMAS JEFFERSON]
Notes on the State of Virginia; Written in the Year 1781, Somewhat Corrected and Enlarged in the Winter in 1782, for the Use of a Foreigner of Distinction . . .
[Paris: Pierres,] 1782 [i.e. 1785]

Jefferson collected materials on Virginia over a period of many years, beginning long before this compilation was requested in 1780. Unpretentious in form and often statistical in character, the work continues to provide useful information on the geography, manufactures, and social and political life of eighteenth-century Virginia.

The date 1782 represents the year when the earliest version of the manuscript reached François Marbois, the French diplomat who had sent questions to several states in 1780. Jefferson continued enlarging it until he handed it to the printer in Paris in 1784 while he was serving as Minister to France. Even then, hoping Virginia would eliminate slavery, he did not have it published, but merely printed in an edition of two hundred copies. However, some nineteen editions were later published during his lifetime. This copy is inscribed on the front flyleaf, "for the honble John Jay from Th. Jefferson."

194. [THOMAS JEFFERSON]
Observations sur la Virginie.
Paris: Barrois, 1786.

The first commercially published edition of *Notes on the State of Virginia* appeared in French, translated by André Morellet, theoretically under Jefferson's guidance. The translation proved a bad one, however, and the author's errata list is long. For the map, suggested by Morellet, Jefferson used his own information for the areas he knew well and relied upon various maps—including those by Scull, Fry and Jefferson, and Hutchins—for geographical details of the frontier regions he did not know. This map remained the most accurate representation of Virginia in the last quarter of the eighteenth century.

195. **THOMAS JEFFERSON**
A Manual of Parliamentary Practice, for the Use of the Senate of the United States.
Washington: Samuel Harrison Smith, 1801.

Jefferson prepared this work while Vice President and presiding over the Senate in the Adams presidency. Subsequently published in many editions and several languages, it still forms the basis of parliamentary procedure in the Senate today. This copy of the first edition contains manuscript notes and an index in two unidentified hands.

196. **SAMUEL JOHNSON**
Journey to the Western Islands of Scotland.
London: W. Strahan and T. Cadell, 1775.

Johnson and Boswell toured Scotland and the Hebrides in 1773; the former's account of the trip was published two years later, but Boswell did not publish his until after Johnson's death. The sixty-four year old Johnson was not partial to the Scots (apart from Boswell), but he enjoyed the trip, which was the longest he took. His account was commended by Edmund Burke, which pleased the author, but Boswell's is much the livlier of the two. This copy of the first edition has the rare leaf of advertisements for the bookseller John Donaldson.

197. **SAMUEL JOHNSON**
Prayers and Meditations.
London: T. Cadell, 1785.

Johnson for many years composed prayers for special occasions, and a few months before his death was urged by the Master of Pembroke College to publish them. He started to revise them, but grew infirm and entrusted the manuscripts to his friend and attendant George Strahan, Vicar of Islington, who published them the year after his death. This copy is uncut in the original boards.

198. **WILLIAM J. JOHNSTON**
Sketches of the History of Stephenson County, Ill.
Freeport: J.O.P. Burnside, 1854.

Stephenson County was created in 1837 out of Jo Daviess County, where the lead mines around Galena had been flourishing since 1823 and where the population had greatly increased in a short time. Stephenson County, with its seat at Freeport, remained chiefly agricultural. This is the second published Illinois county history (Haines's history of Lake County is the first). At the time of publication, the first white settler in northwestern Illinois was still alive.

199. **ABNER D. JONES**
Illinois and the West, with a Township Map...
Boston: Weeks, Jordan; Philadelphia: W. Marshall, 1838.

Jones gives an honest and optimistic Yankee description of the Illinois frontier, based on his experiences while prospecting there. He recommends immigration to the industrious, but warns that the established settlers from the South will be astonished at the New Englander's careful attention to pennies. The map shows seven railways, with several others proposed. This copy, one of five hundred printed, is in the original cloth.

200. **HENRI JOUTEL**
Mr. Joutel's Journal of His Voyage to Mexico...
London: Bernard Lintot, 1719.

La Salle journeyed down the Mississippi and discovered its mouth in 1682, but when in 1685 he sailed into the Gulf of Mexico, he could not find it again and landed instead in Texas. On his journey eastward he was murdered by some of his men, most of whom met a similar fate at the hands of the Indians. Joutel escaped and made his way across Texas to the Red River and thence by the Arkansas and Mississippi to St. Louis. His journal, considered the most reliable account of this expedition, was first published in Paris in 1713; this is a re-issue with changed title of the first English translation of 1714 and contains the first accurate map of the Mississippi.

201. **JAMES JOYCE**
Ulysses.
Paris: Shakespeare and Company, 1922.

Part of the expatriate literary colony living in Paris, Joyce was supported, encouraged, and subsidized by the American bookseller Sylvia Beach. With her bookshop acting as publisher, *Ulysses* was published on Joyce's birthday, 2 February 1922, and in the next eight years was reprinted ten times. It was immediately hailed as a great book, but copies could not be imported into England or the United States for many years. This is a fine fresh copy in the original wrappers of the first edition of 1,000 copies.

202. **JAMES KENT**
Commentaries on American Law.
New York: O. Halsted, 1826–30. 4 vols.

As Chief Justice of the New York Supreme Court and Chancellor of New York, Kent established the foundations of equity jurisprudence in America. In retirement he wrote his four-volume classic,

Commentaries on American Law. It received an enthusiastic reception and became the authoritative exposition on English equity law in the United States. Kent hoped his work might become the American equivalent of Blackstone. The 12th edition (1873) was edited, with supplementary essays, by the young Oliver Wendell Holmes, Jr., and the work remains "the foremost American legal treatise." A presentation letter (New York, October 11, 1827) from the author to the Hon. John C. Smith is laid in volume one; Smith was a former Yale classmate who became a lawyer and Governor of Connecticut.

203. **FRANCIS SCOTT KEY**
Defence of Fort M'Henry.
[Baltimore, 1814]

The text of the song "The Star-Spangled Banner" was written as a poem by Key on 13–14 September 1814 while watching the bombardment of Fort McHenry, near Baltimore, by the British. As a token of his appreciation of the poem, Judge Joseph H. Nicholson, one of the defenders of the fort, had it set to the tune "Anacreon in Heaven," a popular air used for many patriotic songs of the time. The flag which gave Key his inspiration survived the attack, and is now preserved in the Smithsonian Institution. This copy of the second edition of the broadside printing of the words, and the first with Key's name, is one of three recorded copies (there is only one copy of the first edition.)

204. **[FRANCIS SCOTT KEY]**
"Defence of Fort M'Henry," in *The Analectic Magazine,* IV (November 1814), 433.
Philadelphia: Moses Thomas, 1814.

The first magazine publication of "The Star-Spangled Banner" appeared anonymously in *The Analectic Magazine.* Except for several prefatory lines by the publisher and the omission of the author's name, the poem is the same as other early printings. This copy is in original printed wrappers and uncut.

205. **[FRANCIS SCOTT KEY]**
"Defence of Fort M'Henry," in the *National Songster.*
Hagers-Town: John Gruber and Daniel May, 1814, pp. 30–31.

The *National Songster,* commonly regarded as the first book containing "The Star-Spangled Banner," appeared in November 1814. Published anonymously, the poem is preceded by the comment, "Wrote by an American Gentlemen, who was compelled to witness the bombardment of Fort M'Henry, on board of a flag vessel at the mouth of the Patapsco." This stitched copy is in the original plain wrappers.

DEFENCE OF FORT M'HENRY.

☞ [The annexed song was composed under the following circumstances—A gentleman (*Francis S. Key, Esq. of Georgetown, District of Columbia,*) had left Baltimore, in a flag of truce for the purpose of getting released from the British fleet, a friend of his who had been captured at Marlborough.—He went as far as the mouth of the Patuxent and was not permitted to return lest the intended attack on Baltimore should be disclosed. He was therefore brought up the Bay to the mouth of the Patapsco, where the flag vessel was kept under the guns of a frigate, and he was compelled to witness the bombardment of Fort M'Henry, which the Admiral had boasted that he would carry in a few hours, and that the city must fall. He watched the flag at the Fort through the whole day with an anxiety that can be better felt than described, until the night prevented him from seeing it. In the night he watched the bomb shells, and at early dawn his eye was again greeted by the proudly waving flag of his country.]

*Tune—*ANACREON IN HEAVEN.

O! SAY can you see by the dawn's early light,
  What so proudly we hailed at the twilight's last gleaming,
Whose broad stripes and bright stars through the perilous fight,
  O'er the ramparts we watch'd were so gallantly streaming?
And the rockets' red glare, the bombs bursting in air,
Gave proof through the night that our flag was still there;
    O! say does that star-spangled banner yet wave,
  O'er the land of the free, and the home of the brave?

On the shore dimly seen through the mists of the deep,
  Where the foe's haughty host in dread silence reposes,
What is that which the breeze, o'er the towering steep,
  As it fitfully blows, half conceals, half discloses?
Now it catches the gleam of the morning's first beam,
In full glory reflected now shines in the stream,
    'Tis the star-spangled banner, O! long may it wave
  O'er the land of the free, and the home of the brave.

And where is that band who so vauntingly swore
  That the havoc of war and the battle's confusion,
A home and a country, shall leave us no more?
  Their blood has wash'd out their foul footsteps pollution;
No refuge could save the hireling and slave,
From the terror of flight, or the gloom of the grave;
    And the star-spangled banner in triumph doth wave,
  O'er the land of the free, and the home of the brave.

O! thus be it ever when freemen shall stand,
  Between their lov'd home, and the war's desolation,
Blest with vict'ry and peace, may the Heav'n rescued land,
  Praise the Power that hath made and preserved us a nation!
Then conquer we must, when our cause it is just,
And this be our motto—"*In God is our Trust;*"
    And the star-spangled banner in triumph shall wave,
  O'er the land of the free and the home of the brave.

---

203. Francis Scott Key, *Defence of Fort M'Henry* (1814)

206. [FRANCIS SCOTT KEY]
The Star Spangled Banner.
New York: Geib, [ca. 1816–17]

The early sheet music editions of "The Star-Spangled Banner" are undated and their exact order is uncertain. By general agreement, the Baltimore and Philadelphia editions are considered the first and second, respectively. This copy of the first New York edition shows both music and words under the title "The Star Spangled Banner," priced at 25 cents. After the Spanish-American War the song became the unofficial national anthem, and in 1931 Congress officially designated it the National Anthem.

207. **JOHN MAYNARD KEYNES**
The General Theory of Employment, Interest, and Money.
London: Macmillan, 1936.

Keynes was a bibliophile, patron of the arts, and an intimate of the Bloomsbury circle, but it was his formidable talents as an economist that revolutionized modern economic thought. This, his most important book, analyzes the causes of the world-wide Depression and advocates full employment through new investments and a cheap money policy, including government investment. Immediately controversial, the impact of the book has been permanent. This is a fine copy in its original dust jacket.

208. *Kinsley's.*
[Chicago, 1867]

Crosby's Opera House opened on Washington St. in April 1865, and in the same building was Herbert M. Kinsley's restaurant and caterers. Designed to be "a first class establishment, in which *L'Art de Diner* should be carried to perfection" the main room accomodated 1,500 people at one time, and the restaurant was considered the finest in the city. In addition there were rooms for private parties, and Kinsley had also catered railroad trips for General Grant and President Johnson. Three pages of this 88-page book describe the establishment; the rest contain Kinsley's extensive menu and advertisements for Chicago businesses, many of which have illustrations. It appears to have been issued without a title-page; no other copy has been located.

209. [JULIETTE A. KINZIE]
Narrative of the Massacre at Chicago, August 15, 1812 . . .
Chicago: Ellis & Fergus, 1844.

Although the narrative pretends to give an on-the-spot account of the Fort Dearborn massacre, Mrs. Kinzie had no personal knowledge of it, having come to Chicago in 1833. She colored her second- or third-hand oral history with her own vivid imagination to produce an entertaining story of high literary quality, but one which historians must use with caution. This account became chapters 18–20 in her famous book *Wau-Bun* (1856). The pamphlet is in its original printed wrappers.

210. **RUDYARD KIPLING**
The City of Dreadful Night and Other Places.
Allahabad: A. H. Wheeler; London: Sampson Low, Marston, [1891]

By 1890 Kipling's popularity was already such that his Indian publishers brought out a collection of his minor pieces without his permission. This was suppressed, as was a selection with the same title published the following year. The latter was reprinted in London and contains a slip apologizing for the appropriation of the title of a better-known work by James Thomson, although permission had been given for its use. This copy of the English edition is in its original wrappers.

211. **RUDYARD KIPLING**
The Jungle Book.
London and New York: Macmillan, 1894.

Kipling's fame and reputation rests on his short stories, particularly those laid in India or in jungles. They were written and published while he was living in Vermont, disliking and disliked by his neighbors. The Mowgli stories helped bring his fame to its highest peak. This is an extremely fresh, bright copy.

212. **RUDYARD KIPLING**
The Second Jungle Book.
London and New York: Macmillan, 1895.

Published the year after the first Jungle Book, this volume continues the Mowgli tales. Like the first, it is illustrated by J. Lockwood Kipling, the author's father. This copy is in the original dust-jacket, which carries three of the illustrations.

213. **JOSEPH KIRKLAND**
The Chicago Massacre of 1812 . . .
Chicago: Alhambra Book Co., [1893]

Kirkland, a long-time Chicago businessman and attorney, was also a successful novelist. In 1892 he discovered Darius Heald, whose father Nathan was in charge of Fort Dearborn at the time of the massacre and whose mother Rebekah had written a long account of it. This manuscript was destroyed in the Civil War, but her son gave a long description of it to Kirkland, who published it in a magazine and then wrote this book based largely upon it. He strives to reconcile it with the more inventive but widely popular account by Mrs. Kinzie; historians agree that the Heald narrative is more authentic.

214. *The Land Owner.* Vol. 4–6.
Chicago: J. M. Wing, 1872–74.

John M. Wing began *The Land Owner,* devoted to real estate and building in Chicago, in 1869; it resumed publication after the Fire in January 1872 with volume 4 and continued until 1877. It published numerous articles, many illustrations (some of them folding), various supplements, and many advertisements, and is a mine of information on Chicago's rebuilding. (It also proved a financial gold mine for Wing, who established in his will the John M. Wing Foundation on the History of Printing at The Newberry Library.) Volume 6 appears to have ended in June 1874; volume 7 began in January 1875 in a smaller and less elaborate format.

215. **SIDNEY LANIER**
Poems.
Philadelphia and London: J. B. Lippincott, 1877.

The first book of poetry by the Georgia-born writer. His ballads and lyrics are noted for his attempt to produce in verse the sound-patterns of music, and the arrangements of lines and rhythms are both novel and occasionally strained. Lanier died at 39 in 1881; his collected poems were published three years later.

216. **PIERRE SIMON, MARQUIS DE LAPLACE**
Mécanique céleste, translated by Nathaniel Bowditch.
Boston: Hilliard, Gray, Little, and Wilkins, 1829–39. 4 vols.

Between 1799 and 1804, the Marquis de Laplace published his monumental work providing a mathematical solution to the mechanical problems presented by the solar system—in importance "second only to the *Principia* of Newton." Bowditch completed the translation of *Mécanique céleste* in 1818, but delayed publication until he could finance it and thus control it himself. He had to raise $12,000 to print 500 copies. Thus the four-volume translation and commentary was not completely published until 1839, the year of Bowditch's death. *Mécanique céleste* was Bowditch's most notable piece of scientific work and on its account he was offered, but declined, a chair in mathematics and astronomy at Harvard before publication was complete.

Part of the posthumous fourth volume was also published separately in 1839 by the translator's son, Nathaniel Ingersoll Bowditch, as *Memoir of the Translator,* a copy of which accompanies this set. This biographical account is the most important source of information on Bowditch's life. In original boards with the title printed on the front cover, this presentation copy was inscribed to the Hon. Benjamin Gorham and signed by the author on July 18, 1839. (Gorham was a former congressman from Massachusetts.) The bookplates of Alfred and Mary Bowditch appear in the four-volume set.

217. **CHAUNCEY LEE**
The American Accomptant . . .
Lansingburgh: William W. Wands, 1797.

The Spanish dollar (peso) was the unit of currency most familiar in the American colonies, and in 1782 Jefferson proposed it as the unit for the United States. The suggestion was adopted by the Continental Congress in 1785, but it did not come into use until 1794. The dollar sign may have been adapted from the peso; this is its first appearance in a book, in a form somewhat different from what it later became.

218. **HENRY LEE**
A Funeral Oration, on the Death of General Washington . . .
Philadelphia: John Hoff, 1800.

Washington's death on 14 December 1799 caused a great flood of funeral orations. This, by Major-General Henry Lee, member of Congress from Virginia, was delivered at the request of the Congress. It contains the words "First in war—first in peace—and first in the hearts of his countrymen," soon to become famous throughout the country. (They also appear on the monument illustrated in the engraved frontispiece.) This copy is in the original dark blue coated wrappers with printed label, and is a presentation copy from Lee's second wife to their son.

219. **ROBERT E. LEE**
Manuscript of General Order No. 9, signed.
Virginia, 10 April 1865. 1 p.

Following days of desperate fighting and heavy losses, Lee informed the Confederate government on 2 April 1865 that he could hold Petersburg no longer, and withdrawal began that night. After an exchange of messages with Grant, Lee surrendered his Army of Northern Virginia at Appomattox on 9 April. Grant proposed generous terms, to which Lee readily agreed, and on the following day Lee issued his General Order No. 9 to his commanders, confirming that "officers and men can return to their homes" and thanking them for their service. There are a number of copies of this Order; this one was by tradition written for a member of Lee's staff.

220. **JACQUES LE MOYNE DE MARGUES**
Brevis narratio eorum quae in Florida Americae...
Frankfort: Theodor de Bry, 1591.

The second part of De Bry's great collection of voyages, this is a fundamental book for the history of Florida because the Le Moyne narrative is here printed for the first time. The large map is the first to show the French colony, and the plates of Florida scenes and life engraved by De Bry after Le Moyne's drawings are vivid and authentic. This copy, bound by Sangorski and Sutcliffe in full morocco, lacks the leaf of colophon to the plates, as do most copies.

221. *A Letter to the Right Honourable Lord Camden on the Bill for Restraining the Trade and Fishery of the Four Provinces of New England.*
London: T. Cadell, 1775.

Between the Stamp Act and the beginning of the Revolution a veritable flood of pamphlets appeared on both sides of the Atlantic. In 1775 alone, 160 pamphlets were addressed to the British public. The anonymous author of this one takes issue with Lord Camden, the former Lord Chancellor, who steadfastly opposed the taxation of the American colonies. He writes approvingly of Brigadier-General Timothy Ruggles of Boston who the previous year had formed a Loyalist Association to resist any unconstitutional assemblies (and who during the Revolution was banished by Massachusetts, had his lands confiscated, and eventually settled in Nova Scotia).

222. **MERIWETHER LEWIS and WILLIAM CLARK**
History of the Expedition... to the Sources of the Missouri, Thence across the Rocky Mountains and down the River Columbia to the Pacific Ocean...
Philadelphia: Bradford and Inskeep; New York: Abm. H. Inskeep, 1814. 2 vols.

The Lewis and Clark expedition of 1804–6 was the most significant transcontinental journey in American history and is one of the epics of exploration. The expedition was planned by President Jefferson even before the Louisiana Purchase of 1803; the result excited the imagination of the civilized world and opened up the continent to further exploration and eventual settlement. Nicholas Biddle (and later Paul Allen) prepared the history from the manuscript journals, supplemented by oral information. This is one of 22 copies known in the original boards.

223. **ABRAHAM LINCOLN**
Speech of the Hon. Abram Lincoln ... Springfield, Illinois, June 26th, 1857.
[Springfield? 1857]

In reply to a speech by Stephen A. Douglas two weeks earlier (a copy of which is in the collection), Lincoln offers his own differing opinions on the subjects of Utah, Kansas, and the Dred Scott decision. His fundamental differences with Douglas would be more fully developed the following year in the Lincoln-Douglas debates. This copy of the speech, printed in seven pages on one sheet, is unstitched and unopened.

224. **ABRAHAM LINCOLN**
Inaugural Address of the President of the United States ...
[Washington, 1861]

Following Lincoln's election in November 1860, southern states began seceding in December, and the Confederacy was formed in February 1861. In this state of crisis Lincoln was inaugurated on 4 March. In his inaugural address he pledged to uphold slavery in the southern states, enforce the fugitive slave law, and preserve the union. This last was provocation enough for the newly formed Confederacy; South Carolina troops fired on Fort Sumter on 12 April, and the Civil War began. This is one of several contemporary editions.

225. **ABRAHAM LINCOLN**
General Orders No. 1: ... A Proclamation.
Washington, 1863.

Lincoln prepared his Emancipation Proclamation in July 1862, and in September issued a preliminary declaration that on 1 January 1863 slaves in areas "in rebellion against the United States" would be free. On that date the definitive Proclamation was issued. This edition, though long thought to be the first, is in fact the fifth issued in the course of a few days.

226. MARY JOHNSON BAILEY LINCOLN
Mrs. Lincoln's Boston Cook Book ... by Mrs. D. A. Lincoln.
Boston: Roberts Brothers, 1884.

Having directed the Boston Cooking School, established in 1879, Mrs. Lincoln arranged her material in an orderly plan and set forth her recipes in plain, sensible language. Her greatest accomplishment was the standardization of cooking measurements which are still used today. The book became America's standard kitchen companion and is the direct forebear of the even more influential *Fannie Farmer,* which has sold—and continues to sell—millions of copies. This copy is in the original publisher's binding.

227. JOHN LOCKE
An Essay Concerning Humane Understanding ...
London: Thomas Basset, 1690.

Locke's essay led J. S. Mill to call him "the unquestioned founder of the analytic philosophy of mind." The importance of few philosophical books has been so quickly recognized. It passed through many editions in English and was several times translated. This is the first issue of the first edition.

228. JACK LONDON
The Call of the Wild.
New York: Macmillan, 1903.

In 1897 London joined the gold rush to the Klondike and came to know the country and the men which were to be the subjects of his best books. His first collection of stories, *The Son of the Wolf,* brought him national fame in 1900. This, his best and best-known book, was an instant success and has remained enduringly popular.

229. HENRY WADSWORTH LONGFELLOW
The Courtship of Miles Standish and Other Poems.
Boston: Ticknor and Fields, 1858.

Longfellow's popularity, fed by *Evangeline, Hiawatha,* and other poems, was enormously high in the last century, both in America and in Europe. Of this book more than 15,000 copies were sold during the first day of publication in Boston and London. It tells the story of Miles Standish, John Alden, and Priscilla, and is the source of "Why don't you speak for yourself, John?" The central theme, though based on history, is apocryphal, but has entered the American consciousness. This copy has tipped in the front a leaf of advertisements for the publisher's edition of the Waverley Novels.

230. HENRY WADSWORTH LONGFELLOW
Tales of a Wayside Inn.
Boston: Ticknor and Fields, 1863.

The first of three collections of a series of narrative poems told by different travelers, a concept derived from Chaucer and Boccaccio. The setting is a real inn (still standing) near Boston; the characters are based on Longfellow's friends. The first tale is "Paul Revere's Ride," which, though often at variance with history, crystallized an American legend.

231. [AUGUSTUS B. LONGSTREET]
Georgia Scenes, Characters, Incidents, &c. in the First Half Century of the Republic. By a Native Georgian.
Augusta: S.R. Sentinel Office, 1835.

This is the first and best-known book by Longstreet, a Georgia jurist, newspaper publisher, and educator. It is a series of eighteen humorous, realistic sketches of life in Georgia and was the forerunner of works by later writers such as J.G. Baldwin, G.W. Harris, and Mark Twain. The author aimed to "supply a chasm in history which has been overlooked—the manners, customs, amusements, wit, dialect, as they appear in all grades of society." This copy is in its original boards with cloth spine and paper label.

232. [AUGUSTUS B. LONGSTREET]
Georgia Scenes, Characters, Incidents, &c. in the First Half Century of the Republic. By a Native Georgian. Second edition.
New-York: Harper & Brothers, 1840.

To this "second edition" of *Georgia Scenes* (actually a reprinting from the same plates) are added a number of illustrations and a "Note by the Publisher" stating that despite the "urgent demands for a new edition," they have been unable to persuade the author to revise the book, and therefore "have printed a small edition." It was never revised and went through many later printings.

233. [JAMES RUSSELL LOWELL]
The Biglow Papers, edited . . . by Wilbur Homer, A.M.
Cambridge: George Nichols, 1848.

Lowell, descendent of a distinguished New England family, under the influence of his strongly abolitionist wife, revised his conservative opinions, particularly on political questions. The year 1848 marked his most important early writing, which included the second volume of his *Poems* and the first series of *The Biglow Papers*, satirical verses in opposition to the Mexican War. Purportedly written by the young farmer Hosea Biglow and edited by the "Pastor of the First Church in Jaalam," the nine "letters" include three from Hosea's friend, Birdofredom Sawin. This copy is in glazed yellow paper boards.

234. **JAMES RUSSELL LOWELL**
Ode Recited at the Commemoration of the Living and Dead Soldiers of Harvard University, July 21, 1865.
Cambridge: Privately Printed, 1865.

On the greatest day Harvard had yet seen, it paid tribute to the 590 alumni who had enlisted in the Civil War, and even more to the 99 sons who died in the conflict. All else of the occasion has long since been forgotten, but Lowell's ode survives. Composed under great stress, it was not finished until the day itself. Lowell had fifty copies printed, and on 3 September wrote presentation inscriptions; this copy is inscribed to S. H. Gay, then managing editor of the New York *Tribune* and formerly a leading anti-slavery exponent.

235. **[JAMES RUSSELL LOWELL]**
The Biglow Papers: Second Series.
Boston: Ticknor and Fields, 1867.

Written for the *Atlantic Monthly* during the Civil War, these poems and prose pieces continue some of the characters introduced in the first series, this time used in criticizing England's part in the Civil War and stating the patriotic sentiments of Northerners.

236. **WILLIAM H. McGUFFEY**
The Second Eclectic Reader for the Younger Classes in Schools . . .
Cincinnati: Truman and Smith, [1836]

McGuffey, professor at Miami University in Ohio, published his *First* and *Second Readers* in 1836; they immediately became so popular that the advertisement in this copy could say, "The 'Eclectic Readers' have been published three months. In that time four editions have been disposed of, and the demand is continually increasing." Well adapted to the age and capacity of the learner, the *Readers* eventually sold a million copies a year from 1852 to 1894, and became synonymous with American primary education.

237. **SALVADOR DE MADARIAGA**
Disarmament.
New York: Coward-McCann, 1929.

The Spanish writer and diplomat was with the League of Nations for a number of years, after which he became professor at Oxford and other universities and was a life-long opponent of Franco. This book is the outcome of six years' experience of international affairs while an official at the League of Nations; it is written from the point of view of a world citizen and presents the case for disarmament at a critical period in history. This copy, acquired by Mr. Ruggles in 1929, was signed by the author in Geneva the same year.

238. **JAMES MADISON**
A.L.S. to Noah Webster.
Washington, 12 October 1804. 7 pp.

In a letter of 20 August 1804 to Madison, Webster lamented Hamilton's recent death and regretted that his eulogist claimed that the "original germ" of the Constitution "was in the bosom of Hamilton," since Webster had "always understood and declared that you made the first proposal, and brought forward a resolve for the purpose, in the House of Delegates of Virginia . . . " He urged Madison "to communicate to me the facts as far as you know them . . . "

After returning to Washington from his farm, Madison, then Secretary of State, replied at length. He modestly disclaims primary responsibility for bringing about the Constitution: "It is certain that the general idea of revising & enlarging the scope of the federal authority, so as to answer the necessary purposes of the Union, grew up in many minds . . . during the experienced inefficacy of the Old Confederation." While Madison does not recall which delegates at the Annapolis Convention (1786) actually proposed a call for the federal Constitutional Convention, "Mr. Hamilton was certainly the member who draughted the address." He concludes, "To trace in like manner a chronicle or rather a history of our present Constitution would in several points of view be still more curious & interesting . . . " In fact his own *Journal of the Federal Convention,* published posthumously in 1840, remains the principal source of information about this momentous gathering whose deliberations were conducted behind closed doors. This letter, by the "father of the Constitution," is an early peek beyond those doors.

Washington October 12. 1804

Sir

I recd. during a visit to my farm your letter of Aug. 20. and hoped that I should in that retirement have found leisure to give it as full an answer as my memory and my papers would warrant. An unforeseen pressure of public business with a particular one of private concerns interesting to others as well as to myself, having disappointed me, I find myself under the necessity of substituting the few brief remarks which the occupations of this place, and the absence of my papers, will admit.

I had observed as you have done that a great number of loose assertions have at different times been made with respect to the origin of the Reform in our system of Fedl. Govt. and that this has particularly happened on the late occasion which so strongly excited the effusions of party & personal zeal for the fame of Genl. Hamilton.

The change in our Govt. like most other important

238. James Madison, A.L.S. to Noah Webster (1804)

88

239. **JAMES MADISON**
Message from the President of the U. States Recommending an Immediate Declaration of War against Great Britain.
Washington City: Roger C. Weightman, 1812.

In this *Message* sent to Congress on 1 June 1812 recommending war against Great Britain, President Madison reviews the American grievances against British actions, especially its Orders in Council (1809); the blockading of the Netherlands, France, and Italy from American carriers; and the continued impressment of American seamen. Congress, like the nation, was sharply divided on the issues involved. By a close margin, it declared war on 18 June 1812 for "Free Trade and Sailors' Rights." This copy is unopened.

240. **ALFRED THAYER MAHAN**
The Influence of Sea Power upon History, 1660–1783.
Boston: Little, Brown, 1890.

Captain A. T. Mahan, naval officer and historian, published his widely-acclaimed study while serving as president of the Newport War College. Based on his naval history lectures, this work was the first study to go beyond traditional battle descriptions. It demonstrates the interrelationship of naval and political history and constitutes the first philosophy of sea power. It won immediate recognition not only in America but also in Germany, Great Britain, and Japan. Mahan himself once remarked that his lectures were nowhere more carefully studied than in Japan.

241. **THOMAS ROBERT MALTHUS**
Principles of Political Economy, Considered with a View to Their Practical Application.
London: John Murray, 1820.

Educated at Jesus College, Cambridge, Malthus became curate of Albury in Surrey in 1798. That year he published his controversial work *An Essay on the Principle of Population,* which influenced social thought throughout the nineteenth century. During his lifetime, Malthus wrote many economic pieces. His *Principles of Political Economy,* though not a systematic treatment of the subject, sums up the opinions that he had on various topics. This copy is in original boards, uncut, with paper label.

242. **EDWIN MARKHAM**
The Man with the Hoe.
[San Francisco, 1899]

    Markham's mother was poet laureate of Oregon City, Oregon, and so it was perhaps natural that when he came across a copy of Millet's painting he was inspired to write a poem of the same name. Though both now seem somewhat sentimental, they had an enormous popularity in their time. Markham's poem was first printed in the San Francisco *Examiner* for 15 January 1899; its first separate appearance was as this large illustrated folio supplement to the *Sunday Examiner* "by reason of universal demand."

243. **EDWIN MARKHAM**
The Man with the Hoe.
San Francisco: A. M. Robertson, 1899.

    This edition is "now first issued in book form, March thirtieth, Eighteen hundred and ninety-nine." This copy, on tinted paper, is signed by the author and dated April 7, 1905. Accompanying it is a typed letter, endorsed by Markham, stating that this edition was irregular and not authorized.

244. **EDWIN MARKHAM**
The Man with the Hoe.
San Francisco: A. M. Robertson, 1899.

    Another copy, this one on white paper.

245. **JOHN MARSHALL**
A.L.S. to John Jay.
Washington, 22 December 1800. 1 p.

    John Marshall, Secretary of State, writes to John Jay transmitting the proferred commission (not present) as Chief Justice of the United States Supreme Court after John Adams's defeat for re-election. Jay had been the first to hold that position, but had resigned to become Governor of New York. Jay's letter declining the renomination is in the collection, as is the exchange of letters on the same subject between Jay and John Adams. Jay's original commission, signed by Washington, is also in the collection.

246. **JOHN MARSHALL**
A History of the Colonies Planted by the English on the Continent of North America, from Their Settlement, to the Commencement of That War Which Terminated in Their Independence.
Philadelphia: Abraham Small, 1824.

Originally published as an introduction to Marshall's *The Life of George Washington* (1804–07), this version was almost completely rewritten. Marshall saw that a biography of Washington would be unsatisfactory without a survey of the colonies, because "that period of our history is but little known." Despite the frequent dependence on secondary sources, the revised and improved edition was a notable achievement and filled a distinct need for a general history of the colonial period. This is a presentation copy from the author.

247. **MASSACHUSETTS COLONY. GENERAL COURT**
The Humble Petition and Address of the General Court ... unto ... Charles the Second.
[London], 1660 [i.e., 1661]

The Massachusetts Colony was intolerant of religions other than New England Puritanism, and Quakers were early martyrs. Three, including Mary Dyer, old friend and supporter of Anne Hutchinson, were executed in 1660. This pamphlet, signed in type by John Endecott, a founder and Governor of the colony who played a key role in the ugly affair, defends the colony's actions against the "open capital blasphemers." It was presented to the King on 11 February 1661 (old-style dating is used in the pamphlet), and was replied to in another pamphlet by the Quaker Edmund Burroughs. This is an untrimmed copy and is bound with a manuscript document concerning a marriage settlement signed by Endecott as witness and dated 15 June 1663.

248. **MASSACHUSETTS COLONY. GENERAL COURT**
By the Great and General Court of the Colony of Massachusetts-Bay: A Proclamation.
[Watertown: Benjamin Edes, 1776]

In the spring of 1775, Benjamin Edes, the radical printer, secretly conveyed his press and types across the Charles River to Watertown. Following his political colleagues, who established the Massachusetts General Court in Watertown while the British were in possession of Boston, Edes issued many broadsides for the provincial government, including this *Proclamation*. Promulgated on 23 January 1776, it accuses "the Administration of *Great Britain,* despising equally the Justice, Humanity, and Magnanimity of their Ancestors; and the Rights, Liberties and Courage of

AMERICANS, have, for a Course of Years, laboured to establish a Sovereignty in *America,* not founded in the Consent of the People, but in the mere Will of Persons a Thousand Leagues from Us . . . " It concludes with the order that it be read at the opening of the courts, at the annual town meetings in March, and by ministers to their congregations. This uncut copy is inscribed on the back "For the Town Clerk of Kittery."

249. **MASSACHUSETTS COLONY. LAWS**
The General Laws and Liberties of the Massachusets [sic] *Colony.*
Cambridge: Printed by Samuel Green for John Usher of Boston, 1672.

This is the third and updated edition of the 1648 codification. It vividly mirrors the religious beliefs, economic conditions, and social life of the Puritan colonists. Laws regarding church attendance are characteristic of the time, and the enactments against "the cursed sect of Quakers" are remarkable. One of the laws regulating Indians states "that no Indian shall at any time *Powaw* or perform outward worship to their false Gods, or to the Devil, in any part of our Jurisdiction . . . and if any shall transgress this Law, the *Powawer* shall pay *five pounds* . . . "

Printed at the expense of Boston bookseller John Usher (later Governor of New Hampshire), it is the first copyrighted work published in America. In May 1673 the Court ruled that Usher had the sole copyright to this work "for at least Seven years, Unlesse he shall have sold them all before that time." The seal of the Massachusetts Bay Colony appears on a preliminary leaf. This copy is in a contemporary binding and contains extensive manuscript annotations by early owners.

250. **MASSACHUSETTS COLONY. LAWS**
Acts and Laws, Passed by the Great and General Court or Assembly of Their Majesties Province of the Massachusets-Bay [sic] *in New-England.*
Boston: Benjamin Harris, 1692.

These laws were passed at the second session of the first General Court held under the Royal Charter of 1692. The Charter added Maine and Plymouth to the Massachusetts Province and provided for a royal governor. This was the lowest period in the colony's history, symbolized by the Salem witch trials (1691–92). In the laws under "Capital Crimes," the punishment for witchcraft is stated thus: "If any Man or Woman be a WITCH; that is, hath or consulteth with a Familiar Spirit, they shall be put to death." Gradually the power of the old party diminished under the new Charter, and the distinctive Puritan "theocracy" became a British colony, or province. This copy is laid in a deerskin wrapper.

251. **MASSACHUSETTS COLONY. LAWS**
Acts and Laws, of His Majesties Province of the Massachusetts-Bay, in New-England.
Boston: Michael Perry and Benjamin Eliot, 1699–1701.

This publication includes the revision of the laws passed at the sessions of the Provincial Assembly held between 1692 and 1701. Bound with the *Acts and Laws* is *The Charter Granted by Their Majesties King William and Queen Mary, to the Inhabitants of the Province of the Massachusetts-Bay in New-England* (Boston: Michael Perry and Benjamin Eliot, 1699). In both works the name of the publisher Michael Perry (who died 9 October 1700) has been inked out. This copy is in old blind-paneled calf and contains the table of contents to the *Acts*.

252. **MASSACHUSETTS MEDICAL SOCIETY**
The Pharmacopoeia of the Massachusetts Medical Society.
Boston: E. & J. Larkin, 1808.

The Boston Medical Society resolved in 1805 to publish a pharmacopoeia, or book describing drugs and medicines and their preparation. As in all early works, most of the ingredients are herbs and minerals. This book describes itself as "the first work of the kind, which has been published in the United States." This copy is uncut and in the original glazed paper boards with printed label.

253. **COTTON MATHER**
Magnalia Christi Americana...
London: Thomas Parkhurst, 1702.

Probably the most learned man in America, Mather knew seven languages and wrote some 450 works. Towering above them all is "The Great Workings of Christ in America," subtitled "The Ecclesiastical History of New-England from its First Planting in the Year 1620 unto the Year of Our Lord 1698." But the book is much more than church history, except in its largest sense; it incorporates some of Mather's sermons, biographies, and historical narratives, as well as accounts of the Indians. Mather aimed at an epic, unified by the triumphs of God in the New World, and such it has become. This copy contains a leaf of advertisements for Parkhurst's books.

254. **COTTON MATHER**
Magnalia Christi Americana ...
London: Thomas Parkhurst, 1702.

   Another copy, this on large paper, without the advertisement leaf.

255. **BILL MAULDIN**
Up Front.
New York: Henry Holt, 1945.

   Mauldin's war cartoons, produced for *The Stars and Stripes* circulated to the fighting army, became an immediate success with the troops. Their cynical but humorous depiction of the typical dog-face G.I. ensured them a welcome on the home front as well when a selection was finally published in book form, with accompanying text. This copy is in its original dust jacket.

256. **FRANKLIN J. MEINE**
Mark Twain's First Story.
[Iowa City]: Prairie Press, 1952.

   Chicago book-collector Franklin Meine wrote a lengthy introduction to the first separate publication of Twain's first story, "The Dandy Frightening the Squatter." Written when Twain was only sixteen, it was first published in the Boston humorous weekly *Carpet-Bag* for 1 May 1852, and takes only two and a half pages of the booklet. This copy is inscribed by Meine to Mr. Ruggles.

257. **HERMAN MELVILLE**
Moby-Dick; or, The Whale.
New York: Harper, 1851.

   Moby-Dick, the closest work there is to the "great American novel," was published when Melville was thirty-two, his sixth book in as many years. Published first in England in three exceptionally handsome volumes under the title *The Whale*, it was published the next month in America in a thick octavo which one reviewer said looked "very like a whale." Both editions contain passages not in the other, and both also contain corrupt readings. It received mixed reviews, and although it had a respectable sale, going through a fourth printing as late as 1871, it was not really "discovered" until the Melville Revival of about 1920. Since then it has become grist for the academic mills and lay people alike ("Moby-Dick" and "White Whale" restaurants seem now the vogue). The book was issued in various colors of cloth; this one is green.

258. **JOHN MILTON**
Areopagitica; A Speech of Mr. John Milton for the Liberty of Unlicenc'd Printing, to the Parliament of England.
London, 1644.

Milton's classic defence of the liberty of the press—which takes its title from the hill in Athens where the Upper Council met—appeared without a printer's or bookseller's name because of the dangers of printing it, without license, in the face of Parliament's order of 14 June 1643. It is the only one of Milton's prose pieces now much read, and quotations from it are as familiar as some of Shakespeare's—"Give me liberty to know, to utter, and to argue freely, according to conscience, above all liberties." This copy has intact the marginal note on page 8, which is often trimmed, and contains the final blank leaf.

259. **JOHN MITCHELL**
A Map of the British and French Dominions in North America...
[London]: Publish'd by the Author, 1755.

This important map, supporting British land claims, was issued at the request of the British government shortly after the outbreak of the French and Indian War in 1754. Mitchell, a physician and botanist, began work on his map in 1750 after returning to London from Virginia; he had access to extensive collections of manuscript maps and geographical reports held in the archives of the British Board of Trade. Basically a political map of eastern North America, it shows the territorial boundaries of the thirteen colonies and the division between French and British possession, as well as roads, towns, Indian villages, fortifications, and topographical features.

The most authoritative cartographic source of its day, Mitchell's map had numerous English, French, Dutch, and Italian editions. Consulted by the American and British peace commissioners to establish the boundaries of the United States after the Revolution, it was later used to settle scores of boundary disputes well into the nineteenth century. This bound copy of the map on eight sheets is the second impression of the first English edition.

260. **[SAMUEL AUGUSTUS MITCHELL]**
Illinois in 1837...
Philadelphia: S. Augustus Mitchell and Grigg & Elliot, 1837.

This is a detailed description based largely on (and without acknowledgement to) Peck's *Gazetteer of Illinois* (1834), and was published to promote the sale of Illinois lands owned by John Grigg of Philadelphia. It contains six "Letters from a Rambler," first published in a Philadelphia newspaper; they were written during the first three months of 1837 and contain valuable descriptions of several Illinois towns. It also contains a folding map of Illinois showing counties, railroads, and stage lines. This copy is the second state (with an error on the title page corrected), and is in its original printed boards.

261. [SAMUEL AUGUSTUS MITCHELL]
Illinois in 1837 . . .
Philadelphia: S. Augustus Mitchell and Grigg & Elliot, 1837.

Second issue, with the cover title reading *Illinois in 1837 & 8.*

262. **JAMES MONROE**
Message from the President of the United States, to Both Houses of Congress, at the Commencement of the First Session of the Eighteenth Congress. December 2, 1823.
Washington: Gales & Seaton, 1823.

In his annual message to Congress, President Monroe declared, "The American continents, by the free and independent condition which they have assumed and maintain, are henceforth not to be considered as subjects for future colonization by any European powers." The threat of Franco-Spanish intervention to regain the rebelling Central and South American colonies and the aggressive behavior of Russia on the northwest coast of America were the direct causes of this position. The significance of this policy statement, however, was not immediately recognized. In the 1840's President Polk reaffirmed the "Monroe Doctrine" and later in the century the principles became more securely established. The *Message,* bound with the Senate documents of the first session of the Eighteenth Congress, is uncut and in original calf.

263. [CHARLES LOUIS DE SECONDAT, BARON DE MONTESQUIEU]
De l'ésprit des loix.
Geneva: Barrillot & Fils, [1748] 2 vols.

One of the outstanding political philosophers of the eighteenth century, Montesquieu spent fourteen years preparing *The Spirit of Laws,* his major contribution to political theory. In this work Montesquieu examined the history of political theory and jurisprudence and introduced a new method in the study of social structures. Montesquieu saw the ideal government as one that divides political authority and promotes liberty. His work later served as an inspiration for the authors of the Constitution of the United States.

264. **MONTGOMERY WARD & CO.**
Catalogue No. 14.
Chicago, 1875–76.

In 1869 Aaron Montgomery Ward conceived the idea of selling goods, at wholesale prices, directly by mail for cash. The first Montgomery Ward mail order catalogue appeared in 1872, listing 163 items. Within three years, the catalogue listing of the "Cheapest Cash House in America" had increased to 3,899 items, and subsequent issues continued to expand rapidly. This new avenue of marketing goods—many other companies soon followed suit—was greatly influential in raising the standard of living for small-town and rural America. This issue is in original printed paper wrappers.

265. **GEORGE MOORE**
Pagan Poems.
London: Newman, 1881.

Shortly after publishing Moore's third book, the publisher went out of business and had the title leaf excised from all remaining copies. (Some of these were later refitted with a fabricated title page, complicating the problem for dealers and collectors.) In the perhaps thirty copies containing the original title page, Moore signed his initials by the imprint; this is one of those copies. In addition, it bears a contemporary inscription "To my friend P Beatty I affectionately send this book as a token of the time I have given to the service of an art we both love and in which I, at least, have failed." Forty years later, on the facing page, he wrote, "I am glad that I did not proceed further into an art in which I was was [*sic*] not destined to succeed. George Moore, September 1921."

266. **[HANNAH MORE]**
Bishop Bonner's Ghost.
Strawberry-Hill: Thomas Kirgate, 1789.

After coming to London in 1774, Hannah More became acquainted with the literary scene and wrote plays, poems, novels, vivid letters, and eventually tracts which led to the founding of the Religious Tract Society. In asking permission to print this poem at his private press at Strawberry Hill (his "gothick" house near Twickenham illustrated on the title page), Horace Walpole was repaying her for dedicating to him her poem *Florio* in 1785. There were two hundred copies printed.

267. **NEW YORK CITY**
The Charter of the City of New-York.
New-York: John Peter Zenger, 1735.

This is the first printed edition of the Montgomerie Charter (received from Governor John Montgomerie in 1730), and the handsomest specimen of printing from Zenger's press. The Charter increased the municipal power by enabling the mayor to appoint subordinate officers with the advice and consent of the Common Council and, with a majority of the Council, to enact or repeal any by-laws or ordinances. On 11 August 1735, five days after Zenger was acquitted of libel charges, the following notice was printed in his newspaper, *The New-York Weekly Journal:* "The printer now having got his liberty again, designs God willing, to Finish and Publish the Charter of the City of New-York next week." The Charter was actually published 19 September and "sold by the Printer" at a cost of three shillings. This copy is sewn in marbled wrappers.

268. *The New-York Weekly Journal.*
New-York: John Peter Zenger, 6 October 1735—20 September 1737.

The second newspaper issued in New York, *The New-York Weekly Journal* was established 5 November 1733 by Zenger. Set up as an anti-administration paper, opposed to William Bradford's *New-York Gazette,* the *Weekly Journal* was critical of the high-handed acts of William Crosby, the royal governor. Arrested in November 1734 and tried for seditious libel the next summer, Zenger was brilliantly defended by Andrew Hamilton and acquitted in August 1735 after spending nearly ten months in prison. The Zenger trial, reported later in the newspaper, is of great importance in the history of the freedom of the press in America. Zenger published the *Weekly Journal* until his death in July 1746. His wife and then his son continued it until 1751, when publication ceased entirely.

269. **SIR WILLIAM NICHOLSON**
An Almanac of Twelve Sports . . .
London: William Heinemann, 1898.

Nicholson studied in Paris and after returning to England developed a revolutionary style of poster art with bold outlines, simplicity of treatment, and striking silhouettes, which he then applied to woodcuts. Whistler introduced him to Heinemann (for whom he created the familiar windmill device), who published his *Alphabet* and the well-known *Almanac of Twelve Sports,* with words by Rudyard Kipling.

270. **FREDERICK LAW OLMSTED**
Walks and Talks, of an American Farmer in England. New edition, revised, with additions by the author.
Columbus: Jos. H. Riley, 1859.

    The future depictor of Southern life, landscape architect, and city planner began his life after Yale as a farmer. In 1850 he started the series of tours which were to draw forth his literary ability by taking a walking tour of rural Britain. Drawn from his notes and first published in New York in 1852, the account of his trip was published in revised form seven years later. This copy has been rebound with the original cloth laid down.

271. **EUGENE G. O'NEILL**
Thirst and Other One Act Plays.
Boston: Gorham Press, [1914]

    Leaving Princeton in 1907 after less than a year, O'Neill spent six years gaining what he called "life experience." He worked as an able-bodied (and often drunken) sailor in Central and South America, Liverpool, and New York. In 1912–13 he suffered a physical breakdown and, in a Connecticut sanitorium, began to write plays based on his developing view of life among the outcast and oppressed. *Thirst,* his first book, was published in one thousand copies in the American Dramatists Series; this is a fine copy in its original dust jacket. Laid in is a T.L.S. of 6 January 1926 to Perriton Maxwell of *The Theatre Magazine,* New York, saying he is behind on his work and unfamiliar with current New York theatre and so unable to contribute an article.

272. **[THOMAS PAINE]**
Common Sense.
Boston: Edes & Gill and T. & J. Fleet, 1776.

    English by birth, Thomas Paine arrived in Philadelphia in November 1774 and published *Common Sense* anonymously in pamphlet form in January 1776. Intending it as a reply to a speech by George III, Paine not only attacked him (calling him a "hardened, sullen-tempered Pharoah"), but also urged the colonies to declare their independence immediately. At a time when others were hoping for reconciliation and even radicals such as Jefferson were reluctant to attack the Crown, the last tie to the empire, Paine provided the popular political reasoning and rhetoric to cut the tie. This work achieved instant success; it has been estimated that some half million copies were sold. This is a copy of the first Boston edition, stitched and uncut as issued.

273. FRANCIS PARKMAN, JR.
The California and Oregon Trail: Being Sketches of Prairie and Rocky Mountain Life.
New-York: George P. Putnam, 1849.

   A member of a prominent Boston family, Parkman early showed an interest in Indian life during his long excursions to the northern woods. At the age of twenty-three he set out from St. Louis for Wyoming along the Oregon Trail with the dual purpose of observing the customs of the American Indian and improving his frail health. Upon his return, in poorer health and with deteriorating eyesight, Parkman laboriously dictated his narrative to his cousin and published it serially in the *Knickerbocker Magazine* (1847–49). Parkman's most popular work, *The California and Oregon Trail* soon became one of the quintessential accounts in Western travel literature.

274. ELIZABETH PALMER PEABODY
Aesthetic Papers, edited by Elizabeth P. Peabody.
Boston: The Editor; New York: G. P. Putnam, 1849.

   Elizabeth Peabody, sister-in-law to both Hawthorne and Horace Mann, shared their interests in social reform and in education. Her Boston home was the scene of the famous conversational classes of Margaret Fuller, and her bookshop was a meeting place for the Transcendental Club. *Aesthetic Papers* contains contributions by Hawthorne, Parke Godwin, and Emerson; but its primary importance is as the first appearance of Thoreau's landbreaking essay "Resistance to Civil Government" on pages 189–211, which did not appear in book form until 1866. "Civil Disobedience," as it became known, asserts that to cooperate with an unjust government is to condone its crimes, a position enthusiastically and even violently taken by some in recent years. This copy is uncut in the original printed wrappers.

275. JOHN MASON PECK
A Guide for Emigrants, Containing Sketches of Illinois, Missouri, and Adjacent Parts.
Boston: Lincoln and Edmands, 1831.

   A Baptist preacher and author, Peck settled in Rock Spring, Illinois, in 1822 as a missionary of the Massachusetts Baptist Missionary Society. Proselytizing on horseback, Peck gathered geographical and statistical information on much of the region. In the introduction to this work, Peck writes, "Having no connection with the business of land speculation, or town sites, which, without intentional misrepresentation, is apt to color and distort facts, he [the author] has aimed to give a plain and unvarnished statement of things." What follows is a detailed account of the topography, manufactures, and settlements of the area accompanied by a folding map of the "Western States."

276. **JOHN MASON PECK**
A Gazetteer of Illinois, in Three Parts . . .
Jacksonville, Ill.: R. Goudy, 1834.

Using descriptions and observations noted in his diary during his travels, Peck was well prepared to compile a gazetteer of Illinois. He followed the same general plan found in Beck's *A Gazetteer of the State of Illinois and Missouri* (1823). Divided into three sections, Peck's work provides a general view of the state, a general view of each county, and a particular description of each town arranged alphabetically. The first edition of his *Gazetteer of Illinois* was 4,200 copies.

277. **[RICHARD PENN]**
Maxims and Hints for an Angler, and Miseries of Fishing . . .
London: John Murray, 1833.

This book contains "Pickwickian" illustrations by Robert Seymour, and it has been claimed that they inspired Dickens to write *The Pickwick Papers*. In any case, Seymour was engaged to make the drawings for *Pickwick* three years after the publication of this book.

278. *The Pennsylvania Magazine; or, American Monthly Museum for July 1776.*
Philadelphia: R. Aitken, 1776.

The first edition of the Declaration of Independence was printed as a broadside in Philadelphia by John Dunlap during the night of 4–5 July and was quickly reprinted elsewhere in the colonies. The sixth and concluding number of Thomas Paine's *Philadelphia Magazine* contains the first printing of it in a periodical (other than a newspaper). It appears on pages 328–30 under the heading "Monthly Intelligence July 4, 1776" and concludes: "Signed by order and in behalf of the Congress, John Hancock, President. Attest. Charles Thomson, Secret."

279. **[SAMUEL PEPYS]**
Memoires Relating to the State of the Royal Navy of England, for Ten Years, Determin'd December 1688.
[London], 1690.

Samuel Pepys (1633–1703), though of humble parentage, was educated at Trinity Hall and Magdalene College, Cambridge. As administrator of the Royal Navy, where he strove mightily to provide the country with an efficient fleet, he became one of the most important men of his day. In the *Memoires,* the diarist's only acknowledged publication, he gives a business-like account of his contribution to the reorganization and reform of the navy. This is one of the large-paper copies of the first edition which were meant for presentation.

280. [SAMUEL PEPYS]
Memoirs of Samuel Pepys ... Comprising His Diary from 1659 to 1669.
London: Henry Colburn, 1825. 2 vols.

The diary of Samuel Pepys opens 1 January 1660 when he resided in Axe Yard, Westminster, and covers the next nine years of his life. Owing to the unfounded fear that he was losing his eyesight, Pepys closed his diary on 31 May 1669 by writing that to end it was as if he were going to his own grave. The diary provides an extraordinary account of Pepys's life and vividly documents the everyday life and governmental affairs of the time. It is a "thing apart by virtue of three qualities which are rarely found in perfection when separate and nowhere else in combination. It was secret; it was full; and it was honest."

Pepys's six-volume manuscript diary remained in shorthand at Magdalene College until 1825, when it was first published in abbreviated form, deciphered by John Smith and edited by Richard Griffin Neville, third Baron Braybrooke. While many other editions followed, the erotic passages remained expurgated until a complete transcription was published by the University of California Press (1970–83). This copy of the first edition is uncut in original boards with paper labels.

281 *The Pharmacopoeia of the United States of America, 1820 ...*
Boston: Charles Ewer, 1820.

Like the *Pharmacopoeia* of the Boston Medical Society of 1808 (also in the collection), this work was sponsored by official societies. In 1817 Dr. Lyman Spalding proposed to the New York County Medical Society a plan for a national pharmacopoeia which entailed conventions of delegates from separate sections of the country, and a final general convention in Washington. This work is the result of that plan, and the first national pharmacopoeia for the United States.

282. **NICOLAS PIKE**
A New and Complete System of Arithmetic Composed for the Use of the Citizens of the United States.
Newbury-Port: John Mycall, 1788.

Nicolas Pike, a teacher and arithmetician, published his treaties in order to provide a system for the United States that "might be calculated more suitable to our Meridian, than those heretofore published." The presentation of material is organized as lessons with a chapter devoted to the then-new federal monetary system. Pike's own work was one of the first American school textbooks to receive wide popularity; it went through eight editions. This copy formerly belonged to the Essex Institute and Carroll A. Wilson.

283. **PHILIP PITTMAN**
The Present State of the European Settlements on the Mississippi; with a Geographical Description of That River.
London: J. Nourse, 1770.

In this work Captain Pittman gives one of the most thorough descriptions of the western country under British occupation following the French and Indian War. He spent five years in the Louisiana Territory exploring and surveying the country and states that his book "was originally wrote at the request, and for perusal only of the secretary of state for the colonies." The important section on the government of Illinois under the French is in parallel French and English. The eight maps and plans, made from Pittman's surveys, include plans of Mobile, New Orleans, Fort Rosalia (Natchez), and Cascaskies (Kaskaskia).

284. **EDGAR ALLAN POE**
The Raven, and Other Poems.
New York: Wiley and Putnam, 1845.

The most important book of poetry published up to its time in America, *The Raven* was issued at one of the frequent low ebbs of Poe's fortunes. It contains "The Conqueror Worm," "The Haunted Palace," and the final and superior version of "To Helen." Issued as a volume in the publishers' Library of American Books (which would the following year issue Melville's first book), this is a fine copy in the original printed wrappers.

285. **EDGAR ALLAN POE**
Tales.
New York: Wiley and Putnam, 1845.

In this volume begins the detective story, with the still-famous "The Murders in the Rue Morgue," "The Mystery of Marie Roget," and "The Purloined Letter." To his previous stories in the vein of "the grotesque and arabesque" Poe here adds "The Fall of the House of Usher," "A Descent into the Maelstrom," and "The Gold-Bug." This copy is the first printing, and is bound in purple morocco.

286. **NATHANIEL P. POOR**
Catalogue: President Jefferson's Library.
Washington: Gales and Seaton, 1829.

After the sale of his "great" library to Congress in 1815, following the burning of the Capitol, Jefferson said, "I cannot live without books: but fewer will suffice where amusement, and not use, is the only future object." Over the next ten years, he assembled a balanced collection of approximately one thousand titles. After his death in 1826, his second Monticello library was sold, to meet estate expenses, on 27 February 1829. The Washington bookseller Nathaniel Poor issued this auction catalogue, arranged on Jefferson's own classification scheme as illustrated on the verso of the title page and priced at 12½ cents. At the sale, *The Federalist*, item 648 in the *Catalogue*, was purchased by Andrew Bigelow and is now part of this collection.

287. **THOMAS POWNALL**
The Administration of the Colonies.
London: J. Walter, 1768.

A graduate of Cambridge University, Pownall served as Governor of Massachusetts from 1757 to 1759. The first edition of his famous *The Administration of the Colonies* appeared anonymously in 1764 and was republished over Pownall's name in five subsequent editions, each enlarged to reflect current developments in colonial affairs, including, in the third and fourth editions, considerations on Parliament's right to tax the colonies. In this work Pownall suggests the formation of a union of the thirteen colonies in order to form permanently "all those Atlantic and American possessions into one Empire of which Great Britain should be the commercial and political center." This is a fine uncut copy of the fourth edition in original marbled boards and is inscribed, "Govr. Pownall presents his Compliments to Ld Hillsborough." Lord Hillsborough was appointed secretary of state for the colonies on 20 January 1768.

288. **THOMAS POWNALL**
A Topographical Description of Such Parts of North America as Are Contained in the (Annexed) Map of the Middle British Colonies.
London: J. Almon, 1776.

Both the map and accompanying text are a new and much enlarged edition of Lewis Evans's map and analysis of 1755. Here the route of Christopher Gist's journey in 1750–51 through Ohio, Kentucky, and North Carolina is first shown on a map. In the Appendix, Gist's journal of his trip is printed in full, and extracts are given from Captain Henry Gordon's journal of his trip from Fort Pitt to Illinois in 1766. This is a large-paper copy, uncut, in the original wrappers.

289. **WILLIAM H. PRESCOTT**
History of the Conquest of Mexico.
New York: Harper and Brothers, 1843. 3 vols.

Member of a prominent Massachusetts family, Prescott was educated at Harvard. Even though he lost sight in his left eye in a freak schoolboy accident, and had poor eyesight in the other, he became determined to pursue a literary career. Following a trip to Europe in the years 1815–17, Prescott began collecting historical materials and writing articles and reviews on Spanish history. He spent four years researching and writing *The Conquest of Mexico*. Based on original sources and gracefully written, this work is considered Prescott's greatest triumph. It was published in December 1843, and by 1856 the work was in its 26th edition.

290. **WILLIAM H. PRESCOTT**
History of the Conquest of Peru.
New York: Harper and Brothers, 1847. 2 vols.

After the success of *The Conquest of Mexico*, Prescott began work on a shorter companion piece, *The Conquest of Peru*. He employed the same method as in his other histories, presenting a large, dramatic panorama—this time with Pizarro as its center. Both works have remained important chronicles recording the achievements of the Spanish conquistadores in the New World.

291. **[NATHAN PRINCE]**
An Account of the Constitution and Government of Harvard-College from Its First Formation in the Year 1636 to the Year 1742.
[Boston, 1742]

Prince, a graduate of Harvard College in the class of 1718, was the younger brother of the historian Thomas Prince, whose learning, though perhaps more extensive, was considerably duller in the opinions of their contemporaries. But Nathan's teaching methods at Harvard included numerous ear-boxings of the young New England aristocrats, and his difficult and argumentative personality prevented his election to the Corporation and other senior posts. He disparaged the faculty before the students, and at church services, "appearing often times the worse for Drink," he made faces and gestures at Parson Appleton. Finally in 1742, after long forbearance, the Corporation accused him of "great disturbance of the peace of the College," "rude and ridiculous gestures," and "calling a gentleman a puppy."

To aid in his appeal to the General Court, he prepared this tract on Harvard's government. In the first edition (also 1742, and known in one copy only) the "disorder of his Brain" was all too apparent, and, recovering, he issued this more temperate version. Still, the argument was so absurd the Court refused to listen to it. This copy is uncut and one of a half dozen known to exist; it is inscribed "Tho. Balch's, The Gift of Mr. Fowle, Printer." A later signature is "M. Cutler's."

292. **PROTESTANT EPISCOPAL CHURCH**
The Book of Common Prayer.
Philadelphia: Hall & Sellers, 1790.

The Church of England in the American colonies used the English *Book of Common Prayer.* With independence and the formation of the Protestant Episcopal Church, however, there was a need for a book that would omit prayers for the King and be otherwise more suitable for American use. The first American Prayer Book, ratified at the 1789 General Convention in Philadelphia, shortly after Washington's inauguration, was published there the following year. Closely following the English book, it remained in use unchanged for over a century.

This copy, reputedly George Washington's, is bound in red morocco with small green inlays, elaborately tooled, and with five gilt American eagles on the spine (two facing right and three facing left). It is a fine example of American binding done by James Muir of Philadelphia. Its elegant design gives credence to the tradition that it belonged to the first President, a devout Churchman who served as Vestryman at three parishes in Fairfax County, Virginia, and regularly attended St. Paul's Chapel, New York, and Christ Church, Philadelphia, when the federal government was located in those cities. The Prayer Book was owned by the distinguished collectors Winthrop Sargent, Albert Bierstadt, S. L. M. Barlow, and the Rev. Morgan Dix, who noted that it was used in the service commemorating Washington's inauguration in 1889.

292. *The Book of Common Prayer* (1790). Supposedly Washington's copy.

293. **JOHN REGAN**
The Emigrant's Guide to the Western States of America; or, Backwoods and Prairies... Second Edition, Revised and Enlarged.
Edinburgh: Oliver & Boyd; Glasgow: R. Griffin; London: Simpkin, Marshall, [1852]

Regan, a teacher from Ayrshire, Scotland, emigrated in 1842 and located in Fulton County, Illinois. He gives, in story form and with considerable dialogue, an account of his life and experiences there, narratives of many trips to different parts of the state, and descriptive matter. Much of it is in the form of letters, and is an entertaining account of the country. It also includes practical advice for emigrants. The title page describes Regan as "now of Peoria," so presumably he arranged to have the book published in Scotland (it was printed in Ayr); though described as the second edition, it is actually the first in book form, as it had appeared previously only in the *Ayr Advertiser*.

294. **JOHN REYNOLDS**
The Pioneer History of Illinois . . . to the Year Eighteen Hundred and Eighteen . . .
Belleville: N. A. Randall, 1852.

In 1800, at the age of twelve, John Reynolds (1788–1865) moved with his family to Illinois, settling near Kaskaskia. In 1814 he set up law practice at Cahokia and entered politics, rising to the governorship by 1830; later he served in Congress and the Illinois legislature. Although Reynolds led an active political career, he is best remembered today for his autobiographical, historical, and political writings. Most of his works were printed on his own press in his law office in Belleville, where he hired unemployed compositors to set the type.

In the introduction to *The Pioneer History of Illinois*, Reynolds states, "This humble attempt at history, must speak for itself; and the only recommendation I can give it, is, I think it contains the truth." John M. Peck, a close friend, wrote most of the chapter entitled "The Religion and Morals of Illinois." Reynolds collected materials from pioneers still living for the sections on the early French communities. He spoke French fluently, his first wife was French, and he preferred that language in his home. Tradition has it that Reynolds always carried a few copies of *The Pioneer History of Illinois* in his pockets, offering them at thirty cents each.

294. John Reynolds, *The Pioneer History of Illinois* (1852)

295. **JOHN REYNOLDS**
Sketches of the Country, on the Northern Route from Belleville, Illinois, to the City of New York, and Back by the Ohio Valley.
Belleville: J. A. Willis, 1854.

After the adjournment of the General Assembly in 1854, Reynolds took this trip with his second wife, Sarah. While there are nineteen chapters, only seven discuss the states east of Illinois; descriptions of Belleville, Springfield, Chicago, and other Illinois cities are given prominence. In the chapter on Chicago, Reynolds remarks that "the citizens of Chicago have acquired talents and energy in business, that cannot be surpassed. They scarcely take time to eat or sleep; and their gait in the street is generally much faster than a common walk." This copy is inscribed "Presented to the Philosophico[?] Society by the Hon. J. Reynolds."

296. **JOHN REYNOLDS**
My Own Times, Embracing Also, the History of My Life.
[Belleville], 1855.

In this long autobiographical account, Reynolds provides one of the best descriptions of frontier life in Illinois as well as a fascinating picture of himself. It is surprising that no one has done a full scale biography of this Illinois frontier character, the epitome of what one historian has called "Traditionalism."

Two of Reynolds's literary friends, John M. Peck and John Russell, assisted in editing the manuscript, and Lyman C. Draper supplied maps for the author's use in his study of the Black Hawk War, for which, as governor, he had called out the Illinois militia. Reynolds marketed the work himself and sent copies to retail outlets in Washington, St. Louis, and Chicago, where many of them were destroyed in the fire of 1857. This copy is signed by the author.

297. **JOHN REYNOLDS**
The School Advocate: An Essay on the Human Mind and Its Education.
Belleville: Harrie L. Fleming, 1857.

A man of strong convictions, Reynolds declares in the introduction, "It is the duty of every citizen to appropriate a part of his time and labors to advance education." From there he proceeds to give a general outline of the human intellect followed by an appeal to the public for education and an account of educational facilities at the time. In the chapter entitled "School Discipline," Reynolds extols the virtues of cleanliness, sobriety, and industry. Commenting on the proper decorum for teachers, he states, "I would respectfully suggest that no teacher should receive a certificate of qualification, whose face, above and below the mouth, is shrouded and covered with hair." This copy is in original printed wrappers.

298. **JOHN REYNOLDS**
Friendship's Offering: A Sketch of the Life of Dr. John Mason Peck.
Belleville: "Advocate" Book and Job Office, 1858.

Peck, the author of several midwestern guide books, two of which are in the collection, was a close friend of Reynolds for almost forty years. In this pamphlet Reynolds praises his deceased friend (1789–1858), who was also an advocate of education, temperance, and patriotism. He writes, " . . . to the memory of a great and good man . . . whom I very much respected and esteemed . . . only a few copies of this work will be published and those at my own expense." This copy is in the original printed wrappers.

299. **JOHN REYNOLDS**
"The Balm of Gilead": An Inquiry into the Right of American Slavery.
Belleville, 1860.

A long-time defender of slavery, which he sought to establish in Illinois, Reynolds supported the Southern wing of the Democratic Party in the late 1850's. In this political tract Reynolds argues that "the right of slave property was secured to slaveholders by the Constitution, . . . and so soon as the Constitution is destroyed in any of its great fundamental principles, slavery being one—the Government under it must also cease to exist." This copy is in original yellow wrappers.

300. **ALICE CALDWELL HEGAN [RICE]**
Mrs. Wiggs of the Cabbage Patch.
New York: Century Company, 1901.

Written at the encouragement of a club of young aspiring writers in Louisville, this story of an old woman who displays courage and a sense of humor in the face of poverty was accepted for publication at once and became a best seller. In the next forty years it sold more than half a million copies, was translated into a number of languages, and became a success as a play and a movie. This is a fine copy in the original pictorial cloth.

301. **JAMES WHITCOMB RILEY**
"The Old Swimmin'-Hole" and 'Leven More Poems.
Indianapolis: Bowen-Merrill, [1895]

Believing his poetry would be more successful if written by "a genius known to fame," the Hoosier Poet in 1877 wrote "Leonainie" which he had a friend copy out in the hand of Edgar Allan Poe, and which he then proceeded to "discover." It was such a successful hoax that some refused to believe his authorship; in any case his career was launched. Riley's books are marked by Hoosier dialect, simple sentimentality, whimsical kindliness, and frequent pathos. They were enormously popular, and he became perhaps the most financially successful poet of all time, earning and keeping over three million dollars. *"The Old Swimmin'-Hole,"* which includes the famous "When the Frost Is on the Punkin," was the first of his books, published in 1883; this edition of 1895 (with an added essay on dialect) was limited to 100 copies and is signed by him and dated Feb. 26, 1896; it also bears a verse in his hand ("My religion is to jest") signed with his pseudonym, "Benj. F. Johnson, Boone Co., Indiana."

302. **FRANKLIN D. ROOSEVELT**
State of War between the United States and the Japanese Empire.
[Washington, 1941]

Roosevelt addressed a joint session of Congress on 8 December 1941 telling of the attack the previous day on Pearl Harbor and requesting Congress to declare war on the Japanese Empire. It was published as House Document 453 and contains Roosevelt's phrase "a day which will live in infamy." This document ushered in America's participation in World War II, which began in Europe in 1939.

303. **MARY ROWLANDSON**
A True History of the Captivity & Restoration of Mrs. Mary Rowlandson, a Minister's Wife in New-England . . .
London: Joseph Poole, 1682.

"On the tenth of February, 1675, came the Indians with great numbers upon Lancaster." So begins the first New England captivity narrative, that of the wife of the Rev. Joseph Rowlandson, who with her three children was abducted and spent eighty-three days with the Indians before their redemption. Her account is vigorous, and it proved so enduringly popular that it went through thirty editions in 250 years. Indian captivities, an indigenous American genre, were compulsive reading, and many of them, published in pamphlet format, were read to tatters. The first (Boston) edition of the Rowlandson captivity is known by only four

A TRUE HISTORY
OF THE
Captivity & Restoration
OF
Mrs. MARY ROWLANDSON,
A Minister's Wife in *New-England*.

Wherein is set forth, The Cruel and Inhumane Usage she underwent amongst the *Heathens*, for Eleven Weeks time: And her Deliverance from them.

Written by her own Hand, for her Private Use: And now made Publick at the earnest Desire of some Friends, for the Benefit of the Afflicted.

Whereunto is annexed,

A Sermon of *the Possibility of God's Forsaking a People that have been near and dear to him.*

Preached by Mr. *Joseph Rowlandson*, Husband to the said Mrs. *Rowlandson*: It being his Last Sermon.

Printed first at *New-England*: And Re-printed at *London*, and sold by *Joseph Poole*, at the *Blue Bowl* in the *Long-Walk*, by *Christs-Church* Hospital. 1682.

303. *A True History of the Captivity & Restoration of Mrs. Mary Rowlandson* (1682)

leaves; the second survives in only three copies; and of this present London edition about a dozen are known, many of them (as this one) slightly imperfect. (This copy also lacks the appended sermon which occupies pages 35–46.)

304. [ELI FAYETTE RUGGLES]
Recollections of a Busy Life.
[Chicago: H. L. Ruggles, 1904?]

Born near Norwalk, Ohio, in 1833, Eli Ruggles moved with his family in 1838 to a still-unnamed township (later called Hartford) in Van Buren County, Michigan, when there were but four settlers already there. The first and most interesting part of the book is an account of his youthful experiences on the frontier; then in 1861 he attended the Republican Convention in Chicago and got married. Later he and his wife and family moved to Decatur (also in Van Buren County), then far north to Houghton Lake, and eventually (he is vague on dates) to Oak Park, Illinois. Such personal accounts of ordinary citizens are of great interest to historians; this was published privately by his son Harry Lyman Ruggles, owner of a Chicago printing company, probably in the year of his father's death. Only one other copy is recorded in a public library.

305. **THOMAS RUGGLES**
The Usefulness and Experience of Soldiers as Discovered by Reason and Experience . . .
New London: T. Green, 1737.

When the pulpit of the Congregational Church in Guilford, Connecticut, became vacant on the death of his father, Ruggles (Yale College class of 1723) was called to the position. There was considerable opposition eventuating in a separation of the congregation. Though possessed of little brilliance or eloquence, he was a man of strong good sense and practical judgment, and a friend to free enquiry. He is said to have written the best vindication of the Saybrook Platform, and he wrote a history of Guilford. He published four sermons, of which this, his first, preached to an artillery company on 25 May 1736 and "made publick at their earnest desire and charge," is described by his biographer as "written in a sprightly style."

306. **JOHN RUSKIN**
The Stones of Venice.
London: Smith, Elder, 1851–53. 3 vols.

Writer, poet, critic, and artist, and later interested in economics, education, labor, and social reform in general, Ruskin did more than any writer to influence Victorian taste. After the success of his *Seven Lamps of Architecture,* he went to Venice in 1849 wishing to apply his general principles of the rise and fall of the working of moral and spiritual forces to Venetian architecture; the result was three large illustrated volumes. Too heavy to be well supported by their bindings, they are here present in very fine condition; there is an errata slip in volume one, and the advertisements are dated 1853.

307. **JOHN SAPPINGTON**
The Theory and Treatment of Fevers . . .
Arrow Rock: Published by the author, 1844.

Sappington arrived in Saline County, Missouri, in 1819 and in his early days served as a doctor on horseback, ministering to a country where mosquitoes and malaria were widespread. This fearsome and ubiquitous disease he treated first with Peruvian bark and then—in an experiment—with its derivative, quinine, which was eventually to eradicate the disease in mid-America. His book gives detailed instructions on its preparation and use; over a million of his boxes of pills had been distributed, although it took the medical establishment some time to be convinced. It is the first medical book written by a physician west of the Mississippi. Although locally published books are often scarce, this one must have had a large edition, for many copies are recorded.

308. **JAMES E. SEAVER**
A Narrative of the Life of Mrs. Mary Jemison . . .
Canandaigua: J. D. Bemis, 1824.

Mary Jemison's captivity began in 1758 (not 1755, as the title states) when she was only fifteen. Within a few years she had married and had two children, and from her second marriage she had six more. She lived in upstate New York (after travels into the Ohio country) and ended up only four miles from Geneseo, to which she walked in four days at the age of eighty to spend three more telling her story to Dr. Seaver. She lived until her ninetieth year, seventy-five of them as an Indian.

This is an important example of a popular literary genre in America, the Indian captivity narrative. It vividly illustrates the relatively forgotten phenomenon of contented captives of the Indians who were adopted into the tribes and who adapted to Indian ways. Her narrative has gone through many editions—some of them with additions—and is still in print. This copy of the rare first edition is in its original boards and contains the copyright notice on a separate leaf.

309. **WILLIAM SHAKESPEARE**
Mr. William Shakespear's Comedies, Histories, and Tragedies ... unto Which Are Added Seven Plays ... Fourth edition.
London: H. Herringman, E. Brewster, R. Chiswell, and R. Bentley, 1685.

Shakespeare's collected plays first appeared in a posthumous edition in 1623; three other editions in sixty years made it one of the best-selling large books of the century. Of the seven added plays, first printed in the third edition, only *Pericles* is thought to be partially by Shakespeare, and the other six are considered spurious. The plate of the famous Droeshout portrait, here printed as frontispiece with Ben Jonson's commendatory verses, was sufficiently worn to have been retouched by cross-hatching, and the author's appearance is swarthier than previously, and has a noticeable stubble. This is a fine unsophisticated copy of the issue with the "Chiswell" imprint.

310. **DAVID SILLAR**
Poems.
Kilmarnock: John Wilson, 1789.

Sillar, born the year before Robert Burns, was a neighbor and close friend, and it was to him that Burns addressed his "Epistle to Davy, a Brother-Poet," which contains some of his best-known lines. Burns's *Poems, Chiefly in the Scottish Dialect* was published in Kilmarnock in 1786; Sillar's poetry, also in the Scottish dialect and supplied with a glossary, was issued by the same printer three years later. This is a fine unopened copy in the original boards with printed spine label.

311. **JOHN GRAVES SIMCOE**
A Journal of the Operations of the Queen's Rangers ...
Exeter: Printed for the Author, [1787]

The Revolution was in a very real sense a civil war. Loyalists—"in [whose] ranks were to be found the major portion of the colonists who were endowed with wealth, good birth, and education"—comprised about one third of the population of the thirteen colonies, and a large number of them served in the British forces. The Queen's Rangers, Loyalists under the command of Lieutenant-Colonel Simcoe, were in continuous action during the years 1777–1781. The operations described in the book took place in the vicinity of New York, near Philadelphia, and in the Carolinas and Virginia, until Cornwallis's surrender at Yorktown. The book includes ten elegantly engraved maps and plans; this copy is inscribed, "From the Author." Simcoe later became first governor of Upper Canada (Ontario), which was populated largely by Loyalist refugees, and founded the towns of London and Toronto.

312. **F. HOPKINSON SMITH**
Colonel Carter of Cartersville.
Boston and New York: Houghton, Mifflin, 1891.

A native of Baltimore, Smith was an engineer with an avocation for painting until, at age fifty, he turned to literature. His first books were charming travel sketches illustrated with his own drawings, but it was *Colonel Carter of Cartersville* that made him widely known. A novel in the local-color manner, it tells the story of a Southern gentleman down on his luck. An expatriate in New York, a believer in states' rights, slavery, and the Confederacy, he lives on credit and loans until some land he owns is found to contain coal and he becomes rich. This copy is of the first printing and first binding.

313. **JOSEPH SMITH**
The Book of Mormon: An Account Written by the Hand of Mormon, upon Plates Taken from the Plates of Nephi.
Palmyra: E. B. Grandin, 1830.

Despite its historical anachronisms such as introducing oxen, sheep, and silkworms (as well as the knowledge of iron-smelting) into pre-Columbian America, this work became the Mormon Bible and the foundation of a major movement and an extremely successful church. Only in this first edition is Smith named as author; in later editions (the early ones of which were all revised) his name appears as translator. It contains the preface, which was not reprinted; and it also prohibits polygamy, a doctrine later reversed. This copy is bound in contemporary calf with leather label.

314. **[WILLIAM SMITH]**
An Account of the Proceedings of the Ilinois [sic] *and Ouabache Land Companies . . .*
Philadelphia: William Young, 1796.

Speculation in frontier lands is as old as the American colonies, and greatly increased after the cession of western lands by the individual states to the central government under the Articles of Confederation. The Illinois and Wabash companies had been formed in the 1770's and merged in 1779. This historical account, by the company's representative in Congress, Provost William Smith of Philadelphia, details the purchase of lands on the Wabash and Mississippi Rivers from the Indians in 1773 and 1775. Appended is the "Memorial of the Illinois and Wabash Land Company, 13th January 1797." This copy is bound in polished calf by Zaehnsdorf for A. C. McClurg & Co.

315. **TOBIAS SMOLLET**
The Adventures of Peregrine Pickle . . .
London: Printed for the Author, 1751. 4 vols.

Following three years at sea, Smollet returned to London in 1744 and practiced medicine as a surgeon. His first novel, *Roderick Random,* was published in 1748, the same year as Richardson's *Clarissa* and the year before Fielding's *Tom Jones.* The works of all three authors achieved great success. Smollett combines realistic description with the satire of a sensitive observer who is shocked by the brutality and selfishness of human life. *Peregrine Pickle* follows in the same tradition, with power and humor and with rather a lack of general structure. The course of the narrative is interrupted by the long and offensive "Memoirs of a Lady of Quality," written and paid for by the Viscountess Vane, "a woman notorious for gambling and profligacy." This set of the first edition is in contemporary calf, and contains as usual the cancel in Volume III.

316. **HENRY D. SMYTH**
A General Account of the Development of Methods of Using Atomic Energy for Military Purposes under the Auspices of the United States Government 1940–1945.
[Washington],1945.

The development of atomic energy at the University of Chicago and at the Manhattan Project was the most crucial and most secret result of World War II. Smyth produced an informative work which would pass necessary security clearances, and the final result was lithoprinted in 1,000 copies in the Pentagon's facility for reproducing secret documents in August 1945. They were stored in a safe until 11 August, when they were officially released—only a few days after the bombings of Hiroshima and Nagasaki. This copy is without wrappers, apparently as issued, and is accompanied by *The Atomic Bombings of Hiroshima and Nagasaki* and *Photographs of the Atomic Bombings of Hiroshima and Nagasaki,* both by the Manhattan Engineer District.

317. **EDMUND SPENSER**
The Faerie Queen; the Shepheards Calendar; Together with the Other Works of England's Arch-Poet . . .
[London]: Mathew Lownes, 1611.

The Shepheards Calendar, the first of Spenser's important works, was published in 1579 to an enthusiastic audience. The *Faerie Queen,* his greatest work and the epitome of English Renaissance lyric poetry, was begun the same year and finally published in 1590 and 1596. This is the first collected edition of Spenser's works; it economically uses sheets left over from the 1609 folio edition of the *Faerie Queen;* this copy has the second title page dated 1613, and contains the "Mother Hubberd's Tale" which was added to copies issued after the death of Sir Robert Cecil (whose father was the subject of the satire) in 1612.

318. **GERTRUDE STEIN**
The Geographical History of America...
New York: Random House, [1936]

Concerned with creating a new style in an attempt to be peculiarly American, Gertrude Stein wrote experimental prose which excited some literary critics (including Thornton Wilder, who wrote an introduction to this book), but precluded the general popularity she thought she deserved. Despite the large success of her *Autobiography of Alice B. Toklas* (1934), which was written in a witty and more accessible manner, and her triumphant lecture tour of the United States, this book sold under 200 copies of the edition of 1,000; the rest were pulped.

319. **JOHN STEINBECK**
The Moon Is Down.
New York: Viking Press, 1942.

Steinbeck established his reputation in the 1930's with his moving novels of the landless farm-laborer, culminating with *The Grapes of Wrath* (1939). With the advent of World War II he began his war novels; *The Moon Is Down* is about the Norwegian resistance to the Nazi occupation. This copy, in its dust jacket, is of the issue "printed by the Haddon Craftsmen."

320. **ANN SOPHIA STEPHENS**
Malaeska: The Indian Wife of the White Hunter.
New York: Irwin P. Beadle [1860]

The first of the Beadle Dime Novels, *Malaeska* is important not so much for itself as for what it started. Beadle and his brother Erastus had a success with a dime song book and conceived of a series of "dollar books for a dime." *Malaeska* is said to have sold 300,000 copies the first year, and was followed by hundreds of similar works. To them as much as to any other single source may be attributed America's conception of the "Far West" of cowboys and Indians. Bound with this copy are the next five novels in the series. From the library of Frank J. Hogan.

321. [LAURENCE STERNE]
The Life and Opinions of Tristram Shandy.
[York]; London: R. and J. Dodsley [etc.], 1760–67. 9 vols.

Sterne published the first two volumes of his literary curiosity *Tristram Shandy* in 1760, and finally completed it—in nine volumes—in 1767. It has the distinction of being denounced by Johnson, Richardson, Walpole, and Goldsmith on both literary and moral grounds. Despite the title, the book gives little of the life, and nothing of the opinions, of the nominal hero, who gets born only in volume four and soon disappears from the story altogether. Instead there are humorous figures who are chiefly occupied with exposing the author's personality and whimsical imagination in many digressions. Physically the book is whimsical too, providing a leaf of marbled paper (an "emblem of my work!"), a blank leaf for an imaginary portrait, and an entire blank section. This set is of the first issue of the first two volumes, has the half titles where called for, and has the author's signature in Volumes V, VI, and IX.

322. **HARRIET BEECHER STOWE**
Uncle Tom's Cabin; or, Life among the Lowly.
Boston: John P. Jewett; Cleveland: Jewett, Proctor, & Worthington, 1852. 2 vols.

Mrs. Stowe began her novel with the death scene of Uncle Tom, the reading of which caused her children to cry. The book was serialized in the abolitionist journal *The National Era;* instead of concluding in a few numbers, it ran on until when published in book form it appeared in two volumes. More than 300,000 copies were sold in America and twenty editions appeared in England the same year. It had enormous influence, and well-known is Lincoln's remark, "So this is the little woman who wrote the book that made this big war." Accompanying this set is a signed note replying to a request for a signature.

323. [JONATHAN SWIFT]
A Tale of a Tub . . . to Which Is Added an Account of a Battel between the Antient and Modern Books in St. James's Library.
London: John Nutt, 1704.

Irish born and educated, Swift entered the household of Sir William Temple at Moor Park, Surrey, in 1689. Ordained in Ireland in 1694, he returned to Temple and wrote both *A Tale of a Tub* and *The Battle of the Books,* which were published together in 1704. The latter is a satire directed at a subject Temple had treated in his essay on the comparative merits of ancient and modern learning; the former is a satire on corruption in religion, with frequent digressions on subjects including madness, an early example of Swift's love of paradox and of his misanthropy. In this copy a contemporary binder has misbound two preliminary leaves at the end.

324. [JONATHAN SWIFT]
Travels into Several Remote Nations of the World, by Lemuel Gulliver ...
London: Benj. Motte, 1726. 2 vols.

After the death of Sir William Temple in 1699, and discouraged by prospects for preferment in England, Swift returned to Ireland, where he became Dean of St. Patrick's Cathedral in 1713. He fell in love but never married, and wrote a very large number of pamphlets on political, religious, and Irish affairs. Only for *Gulliver's Travels*, his most extensive work, did he receive any payment (£200). Gulliver's adventures in Lilliput, among the Brobdingnagians, and with the Houyhnhnms, appeal now as then to both old and young as a powerful satire on man and human institutions, and as a fascinating adventure tale. In this copy of the first edition the portrait in Volume I is in the first state, and page 64 of part 4 is in the second (cancelled) state.

325. **BOOTH TARKINGTON**
The Gentleman from Indiana.
New York: Doubleday & McClure, 1899.

Born in Indianapolis in 1869, Tarkington was educated at Exeter, Purdue, and Princeton, where he was editor, writer, and illustrator for several student publications. *The Gentleman from Indiana*, his first book, was a success, and he went on to write many others about life in the Middle West, of which two won Pulitzer Prizes. This copy is in a fine bright binding, with the spine (and the text) in the first state.

326. **BOOTH TARKINGTON**
Penrod.
Garden City: Doubleday, Page, 1914.

Tarkington is also noted for his books about boys and adolescents, of which *Penrod* is the best known. The delightful and humorous narrative tells of the typical adventures of a twelve-year-old boy, who is involved in characteristic frays and scrapes and carries on an active warfare with his parents and teachers: "You don't expect boys to be civilized, do you?" The first edition was of 20,000 copies, and five other printings followed the same year. This copy is of the first state.

327. **BANNASTRE TARLETON**
A History of the Campaigns of 1780 and 1781 in the Southern Provinces of North America.
London: T. Cadell, 1787.

Tarleton's *History,* including four battle plans and a map of "The Marches of Lord Cornwallis in the Southern Provinces," contains many important documents. Although portions of the work are historically accurate, the narrative is marred by the vanity of the author, who distorts some events to place his own services in a more favorable light. Tarleton's unjust criticism of Cornwallis called forth a caustic review by Roderick McKenzie in his *Strictures on Lieutenant-Colonel Tarleton's History* (1787).

It is likely that Tarleton was assisted in this compilation by others, among them Mary Robinson, "the Exquisite Perdita." A famous actress, author, and mistress of King George IV when Prince of Wales, Robinson and Tarleton lived together for several years. This copy is inscribed twice: the title page reads "From the Author to his dear Mary" and the front flyleaf bears the note "This book belongs to Mrs. Robinson, No. 14 St. James's Place."

328. *The Tatler, by Isaac Bickerstaff.*
Numbers 1 (12 April 1709)—272 (2–4 January 1711)
London, 1709–11.

The first great English literary periodical, *The Tatler* started as a folio half-sheet issued three times a week. Of the first 271 issues, 188 were by Richard Steele, 42 by Joseph Addison, and 36 were written jointly. Other contributors probably included Alexander Pope and certainly included Jonathan Swift, who invented the character taken over by Steele. Although the paper was brought to an end with number 271, various publishers immediately stepped in to fill the gap. Present with this set is number 272 issued by John Baker, which contains high praise for Steele.

329. **[ALFRED, LORD TENNYSON]**
Poems, by Two Brothers.
London: W. Simpkin and R. Marshall, 1827.

Despite the title, all three Tennyson brothers contributed to this book, Tennyson's first, published when he was eighteen. Frederick contributed only three or four poems; the rest are by Alfred and Charles. Although they pledged never to reveal who wrote which, Frederick, together with Alfred's son Hallam, many years later sought to attribute authorship; forty-two poems are definitely assigned to Alfred. This copy is uncut in the original grey boards with printed label.

330. **[ALFRED, LORD TENNYSON]**
In Memoriam.
London: Edward Moxon, 1850.

Tennyson's intimate friend Arthur Henry Hallam, a young man of extraordinary talent, died in 1833 in Vienna at the age of twenty-two. Tennyson began his elegy the same year, and continued working on it for nearly twenty years. It is considered one of the three great elegies in English poetry, the others being Milton's "Lycidas" and Shelley's "Adonais." It is less a single elegy than a series of poems written at different times and in different moods, as Tennyson adjusted to his loss. The poem describes "the way of the soul" in the presence of a great loss, the gradual acceptance, and finally a spiritual sense of contact with God and humanity. This copy is of the first state of the text.

331. **DAVID THOMAS**
Travels through the Western Country in the Summer of 1816.
Auburn, New York: David Rumsey, 1819.

Thomas made this journey with Jonathan Swan, a merchant of Aurora, New York, for the purpose of exploring the Wabash lands. He spent much time in the Vincennes area, but does not appear to have crossed over into Illinois. The emphasis in the *Travels*, an important account of the early Indiana frontier, is upon natural history, topography, commerce, agriculture, manufactures, and antiquities. This copy includes the folding map "Vincennes District."

332. **ISAIAH THOMAS**
The History of Printing in America.
Worcester: Isaiah Thomas, Jun., 1810. 2 vols.

Printer, historian, and founder of the American Antiquarian Society, Thomas was the country's leading publisher in the last quarter of the eighteenth century. Apprenticed to a printer by the Overseers of the Poor in Boston as a young boy, he was considered an excellent printer by the age of seventeen. A few years later Thomas established his own newspaper, the *Massachusetts Spy,* which he moved to Worcester at the time of the Revolution. Eventually he employed 150 persons in his printing establishment in Worcester, which included seven presses, a paper mill, and bindery. By the time he retired in 1802, Thomas had published over four hundred titles covering numerous subjects. He devoted the remainder of his life to scholarship, and from his personal library he obtained the source material for *The History of Printing in America.* Thomas's work remains the standard authority on printing in the United States from 1640 to 1800. This set is uncut and bound in printed boards and spines.

333. **HENRY D. THOREAU**
A Week on the Concord and Merrimack Rivers.
Boston and Cambridge: James Munroe [etc.], 1849.

Self-styled "a mystic, a transcendentalist, and a natural philosopher to boot," Thoreau made a trip with his brother on the Concord and Merrimack Rivers in 1839, which he wrote up from notes during his residence at Walden Pond in 1845–47. The book describes the scenery and people and maintains a certain air of romantic adventure, but the travel narrative is subordinated to learned digressions into history, religion, philosophy, poetry, and the nature of friendship. A thousand copies of the book were printed at Thoreau's expense, but it did not sell well and in 1853 706 copies were returned to him, to spend the next nine years in his attic bedroom.

334. **HENRY D. THOREAU**
Walden; or, Life in the Woods.
Boston: Ticknor and Fields, 1854.

Thoreau began construction of his famous cabin at Walden Pond, near Concord, the end of March 1845 and moved in on the 4th of July. There he lived alone until September 1847, supplying his needs by his own labor and developing and testing his transcendental philosophy of individualism, self-reliance, and material economy for the sake of spiritual wealth. *Walden,* based on this experience, is now a classic; it is an inspiration to nature lovers, philosophers, and those who like to read English prose written with clarity and style.

335. **HENRY D. THOREAU**
Cape Cod.
Boston: Ticknor and Fields, 1865.

Thoreau made several brief trips during the years 1849–55, which provided material for three books published after his death in 1862. He visited Cape Cod three times and published some chapters in *Putnam's Magazine* in 1855; the book form, containing ten chapters, was edited by William Ellery Channing the younger, an intimate friend and a fellow Transcendentalist. Unlike most copies, this one does not contain the publisher's catalogue at the end.

336. [CHRISTIANA H. TILLSON]
Reminiscences of Early Life in Illinois, by Our Mother.
[Amherst? 1873]

This is one of the rarest and best of the personal narratives of pioneer life in southern Illinois (1819–27). After returning to Amherst, Mrs. Tillson wrote her story "during the last invalid hours of her life, for the entertainment of her youngest child." She died in New York City 29 May 1872. The tone of her *Reminiscences* was intimate and the edition small but, as frequently happens, the book written for the few contains qualities which recommend it to the many. It was reprinted as one of the Lakeside Classics in 1919, retitled *A Woman's Story of Pioneer Illinois.* The book, privately printed, contains four mounted photographs of the Tillson family and their home.

337. **JONATHAN TODD**
Judgment and Mercy ... Two Sermons ... after the Much Lamented Death of the Reverend Mr. Thomas Ruggles ...
New Haven: Thomas & Samuel Green, [1770]

Ruggles (1704–1770) was pastor of the Congregational Church in Guilford, and while there published four sermons, one of which is in this collection. However, his powers failed early, and a colleague-pastor was installed in 1757. Jonathan Todd, of the Yale College class of 1732 (along with Ruggles's half-brother Nathaniel), served the church in East Guilford (now Madison) for fifty years until his death in 1791. These sermons were delivered in Mr. Ruggles's church and published at the congregation's request. This copy, complete with the half title and errata, is stitched and uncut as issued.

338. **RALPH TOMLINSON**
The Anacreontic Song.
London: Longman & Broderip, [ca. 1780]

The rare first issue of the first edition of the English music later adopted for *The Star-Spangled Banner.* The Anacreontic Society, composed of men of wealth, wit, and learning, was founded in 1766. Meetings were held regularly at the Crown and Anchor Tavern in the Strand. After supper it was customary to open the choral singing with the club's constitutional song, *To Anacreon in Heaven.* (Anacreon was a famous classical Greek lyric poet.) It is believed that John Stafford Smith, a noted musician and member of the Society, composed the music. Whether Francis Scott Key wrote his verses with this melody in mind is uncertain, but *The Star-Spangled Banner* was immediately set to it in 1814.

339. **FRANCISCO TURANO**
Logica major. Manuscript, 437 pp.
[Rome? after 1707]

Based on Aristotle's works on logic, this textbook is divided into eight sections. Turano, a Jesuit, appears to have published no books and is not mentioned in the standard bibliography of Jesuit authors. Inserted is a printed folding table dated Rome, 1707, meant to accompany an introduction to Aristotle's *Logic* by Antonio Casilio (or Casiglio), a work first published in 1629 and reprinted a number of times.

340. **UNITED STATES. CONGRESS**
. . . An Act to Provide for the Government of the Territory North-West of the River Ohio.
[New York, 1789]

On 13 July 1787 the Continental Congress passed the Northwest Ordinance (a copy of which is in the collection). One of the actions of the first Congress under the Constitution was to implement the Ordinance so that the territorial government "may continue to have full effect"; the Act provides for the presidential appointment of territorial officers and direct reporting of the Governor to the President. This broadside is uncut.

341. **UNITED STATES. CONGRESS**
. . . An Act to Provide for the Government of the Territory North-West of the River Ohio.
[New York, 1789]

Another issue on large paper with the added Certification of four lines signed in manuscript by the Secretary of the Senate and the Clerk of the House of Representatives. This copy is uncut.

342. **UNITED STATES. CONGRESS**
Journal of the First Session of the Senate of the United States of America, Begun and Held at the City of New-York, March 4th, 1789 . . .
New-York: Thomas Greenleaf, 1789.

Congress, the first body to be established in the new government, antedated the Presidency, the executive departments, and the judicial branch. The *Journal* of the first session (4 March to 29 September 1789) contains the official documents of the Senate which were prepared from the minutes of the Secretary of the Senate. Among many important matters recorded in these proceedings are the Senate debates over seventeen proposed amendments to the Constitution. In late September twelve amendments were passed by the House and Senate; these are appended to the *Journal*. All but two of the amendments were ratified by the states; articles I and II, concerning the apportionment of representatives and congressional salaries, were rejected. When the tenth state, Virginia, ratified them on 15 December 1791, the Bill of Rights went into effect. This copy is uncut.

343. **UNITED STATES. CONSTITUTION**
Plan of the New Constitution for the United States of America...
London: J. Debrett, 1787.

In the spring of 1787 the delegates met at the Constitutional Convention in Philadelphia "for the sole and express purpose of revising the Articles of Confederation." After months of deliberation, they wrote a new Constitution. The official edition was ordered printed on 17 September 1787 for submission to the Continental Congress; it was issued two days later. During the next few months, the Constitution was widely reprinted in the United States. This is a copy of the first London edition, which was also published in 1787 and includes Washington's letter submitting the Constitution to Congress.

344. **UNITED STATES. CONSTITUTION**
Plan of the New Constitution for the United States of America...
London: J. Debrett, 1792.

This "new edition, corrected" appeared five years after the first, indicating a continued interest in the subject.

345. **UNITED STATES. CONTINENTAL CONGRESS**
Journal of the Proceedings of the Congress, Held at Philadelphia, September 5, 1774.
Philadelphia: William and Thomas Bradford, 1774.

First assembled as an advisory council for the colonies, the Continental Congress eventually evolved into the central government. The first Congress met in Philadelphia 5 September to 26 October 1774, with all colonies but Georgia represented, to consider action for recovery of rights forfeited under Parliament's repressive Coercive Acts. Appearing on pages 60–63 is the Declaration of Rights, consisting of ten resolutions including the right to "life, liberty, and property." The title page bears the device of twelve arms and hands, symbolizing the twelve colonies represented, sustaining a column resting on the Magna Carta and surmounted by the cap of Liberty, with the motto *Hanc Tuemur, Hac Nitimur* (This we defend; on it we depend).

346. UNITED STATES. CONTINENTAL CONGRESS
A Declaration by the Representatives of the United Colonies of North-America . . . Seting [sic] *Forth the Causes and Necessity of Their Taking Up Arms.*
Philadelphia: William and Thomas Bradford, 1775.

After the outbreak of hostilities at Bunker Hill (17 June 1775), the Continental Congress issued this Declaration justifying the use of force, which preceded the Declaration of Independence by one year. Jefferson wrote the first version which John Dickinson rewrote and strengthened. The Declaration indicted Parliament for having "attempted to effect their cruel and impolitic purpose of enslaving these Colonies by violence, and have thereby rendered it necessary for us to close with their last appeal from Reason to Arms." Congress approved the measure on 6 July 1775. This is a copy of the first edition, which was widely reprinted.

347. UNITED STATES. CONTINENTAL CONGRESS
A Declaration by the Representatives of the United Colonies of North-America . . . Seting [sic] *Forth the Causes and Necessity of Their Taking Up Arms.*
Philadelphia: William and Thomas Bradford, 1775.

Another copy, lacking the half title.

348. UNITED STATES. CONTINENTAL CONGRESS
A Circular Letter from the Congress of the United States to Their Constituents.
Boston, [1779]

This *Letter,* dated 13 September 1779, explains why the depreciation of currency and a national debt were unavoidable during the Revolutionary War. It concludes by urging citizens "to finish the contest as you began it, honestly and gloriously.—Let it never be said that America had no sooner become independent than she became insolvent . . . in the very hour when all the nations of the earth were admiring and almost adoring the splendor of her rising." Written by Elbridge Gerry, the pamphlet was first printed in Philadelphia and quickly reprinted in Boston "by Order of the General Assembly of the State of Massachusetts Bay," who also ordered (2 October) that it be "sent to the several Ministers of the Gospel in the Towns and Parishes within this State." This uncut copy is addressed to "Revd. Mr. Foxcroft, New Glocester."

349. **UNITED STATES. CONTINENTAL CONGRESS**
Manuscript: "By the United States in Congress Assembled. Octr. 4th 1782."
[Philadelphia], 1782. 4 pp.

During the autumn of 1782, the American Commissioners (Adams, Franklin, and Jay) secretly negotiated and signed the preliminary articles of peace with Great Britain. In these negotiations the American delegation ignored its instructions from Congress "to inviolably adhere to the Treaty of Alliance with his Most Christian Majesty." As stated in this Resolution, Congress had ordered the commissioners to consult and follow the advice of the French and to "conclude neither a separate peace or truce with Great Britain." The Americans did not ultimately violate their treaty obligations with France, since the articles were conditional and became effective only when France and Britain had also concluded peace. The Treaty of Paris was signed 3 September 1783, officially ending the Revolutionary War. This manuscript copy of the Congressional Resolution is signed by Charles Thomson, the "perpetual Secretary" of the Continental Congress.

350. **UNITED STATES. CONTINENTAL CONGRESS**
By the United States in Congress Assembled, April 30, 1784.
[Annapolis: John Dunlap, 1784]

This broadside contains resolutions designed to empower Congress to control exports and imports. It states that "unless the United States in Congress assembled shall be vested with powers competent to the protection of commerce, they can never command reciprocal advantages in trade; and without these, our foreign commerce must decline and eventually be annihilated." The resolutions proposed allowed Congress to prohibit trade with subjects of foreign nations who had not entered into commercial treaties and also to prohibit importations in vessels not of the country in which goods were produced. The failure to achieve consent from the states under the Articles of Confederation to regulate commerce was one of the compelling reasons for the ultimate scrapping of the Articles and the adoption of the Constitution. This copy is inscribed "Chas. Thomson Secy."

351. **UNITED STATES. CONTINENTAL CONGRESS**
An Ordinance for the Establishment of the Mint of the United States of America; and for Regulating the Value and Alloy of Coin.
[New York, 1786]

In 1785 Thomas Jefferson proposed the establishment of a coinage system based on the Spanish milled dollar. His proposal was adopted by Congress, and a full plan of coinage was enacted 8

An ORDINANCE for the GOVERNMENT of the TERRITORY of the UNITED STATES, North-West of the River OHIO.

BE IT ORDAINED by the United States in Congress assembled, That the said territory, for the purposes of temporary government, be one district; subject, however, to be divided into two districts, as future circumstances may, in the opinion of Congress, make it expedient.

Be it ordained by the authority aforesaid, That the estates both of resident and non-resident proprietors in the said territory, dying intestate, shall descend to, and be distributed among their children, and the descendants of a deceased child in equal parts; the descendants of a deceased child or grand-child, to take the share of their deceased parent in equal parts among them: And where there shall be no children or descendants, then in equal parts to the next of kin, in equal degree; and among collaterals, the children of a deceased brother or sister of the intestate, shall have in equal parts among them their deceased parents share; and there shall be in no case a distinction between kindred of the whole and half blood; saving in all cases to the widow of the intestate, her third part of the real estate for life, and one third part of the personal estate; and this law relative to descents and dower, shall remain in full force until altered by the legislature of the district. ———— And until the governor and judges shall adopt laws as herein after mentioned, estates in the said territory may be devised or bequeathed by wills in writing, signed and sealed by him or her, in whom the estate may be, (being of full age) and attested by three witnesses;———— and real estates may be conveyed by lease and release, or bargain and sale, signed, sealed, and delivered by the person being of full age, in whom the estate may be, and attested by two witnesses, provided such wills be duly proved, and such conveyances be acknowledged, or the execution thereof duly proved, and be recorded within one year after proper magistrates, courts, and registers shall be appointed for that purpose; and personal property may be transferred by delivery, saving, however, to the French and Canadian inhabitants, and other settlers of the Kaskaskies, Saint Vincent's, and the neighbouring villages, who have heretofore professed themselves citizens of Virginia, their laws and customs now in force among them, relative to the descent and conveyance of property.

Be it ordained by the authority aforesaid, That there shall be appointed from time to time, by Congress, a governor, whose commission shall continue in force for the term of three years, unless sooner revoked by Congress; he shall reside in the district, and have a freehold estate therein, in one thousand acres of land, while in the exercise of his office.

There shall be appointed from time to time, by Congress, a secretary, whose commission shall continue in force for four years, unless sooner revoked, he shall reside in the district, and have a freehold estate therein, in five hundred acres of land, while in the exercise of his office; it shall be his duty to keep and preserve the acts and laws passed by the legislature, and the public records of the district, and the proceedings of the governor in his executive department; and transmit authentic copies of such acts and proceedings, every six months, to the secretary of Congress: There shall also be appointed a court to consist of three judges, any two of whom to form a court, who shall have a common law jurisdiction, and reside in the district, and have each therein a freehold estate in five hundred acres of land, while in the exercise of their offices; and their commissions shall continue in force during good behaviour.

The governor and judges, or a majority of them, shall adopt and publish in the district, such laws of the original states, criminal and civil, as may be necessary, and best suited to the circumstances of the district, and report them to Congress, from time to time, which laws shall be in force in the district until the organization of the general assembly therein, unless disapproved of by Congress; but afterwards the legislature shall have authority to alter them as they shall think fit.

The governor for the time being, shall be commander in chief of the militia, appoint and commission all officers in the same, below the rank of general officers; all general officers shall be appointed and commissioned by Congress.

Previous to the organization of the general assembly, the governor shall appoint such magistrates and other civil officers, in each county or township, as he shall find necessary for the preservation of the peace and good order in the same: After the general assembly shall be organized, the powers and duties of magistrates and other civil officers shall be regulated and defined by the said assembly; but all magistrates and other civil officers, not herein otherwise directed, shall, during the continuance of this temporary government, be appointed by the governor.

For the prevention of crimes and injuries, the laws to be adopted or made shall have force in all parts of the district, and for the execution of process, criminal and civil, the governor shall make proper divisions thereof——and he shall proceed from time to time, as circumstances may require, to lay out the parts of the district in which the Indian titles shall have been extinguished, into counties and townships, subject, however, to such alterations as may thereafter be made by the legislature.

So soon as there shall be five thousand free male inhabitants, of full age, in the district, upon giving proof thereof to the governor, they shall receive authority, with time and place, to elect representatives from their counties or townships, to represent them in the general assembly; provided that for every five hundred free male inhabitants there shall be one representative, and so on progressively with the number of free male inhabitants, shall the right of representation increase, until the number of representatives shall amount to twenty-five, after which the number and proportion of representatives shall be regulated by the legislature; provided that no person be eligible or qualified to act as a representative, unless he shall have been a citizen of one of the United States three years and be a resident in the district, or unless he shall have resided in the district three years, and in either case shall likewise hold in his own right, in fee simple, two hundred acres of land within the same:—Provided also, that a freehold in fifty acres of land in the district, having been a citizen of one of the states, and being resident in the district; or the like freehold and two years residence in the district shall be necessary to qualify a man as an elector of a representative.

The representatives thus elected, shall serve for the term of two years, and in case of the death of a representative, or removal from office, the governor shall issue a writ to the county or township for which he was a member, to elect another in his stead, to serve for the residue of the term.

The general assembly, or legislature, shall consist of the governor, legislative council, and a house of representatives. The legislative council shall consist of five members, to continue in office five years, unless sooner removed by Congress, any three of whom to be a quorum, and the members of the council shall be nominated and appointed in the following manner, to wit: As soon as representatives shall be elected, the governor shall appoint a time and place for them to meet together, and, when met, they shall nominate ten persons, residents in the district, and each possessed of a freehold in five hundred acres of land, and return their names to Congress; five of whom Congress shall appoint and commission to serve as aforesaid; and whenever a vacancy shall happen in the council, by death or removal from office, the house of representatives shall nominate two persons, qualified as aforesaid, for each vacancy, and return their names to Congress; one of whom Congress shall appoint and commission for the residue of the term; and every five years, four months at least before the expiration of the time of service of the members of council, the said house shall nominate ten persons, qualified as aforesaid, and return their names to Congress, five of whom Congress shall appoint and commission to serve as members of the council five years, unless sooner removed. And the governor, legislative council, and house of re-

---

352. The Northwest Ordinance (1787)

130

August 1786. In this broadside *Ordinance,* dated 20 September 1786, a mint is ordered "agreeably to the resolves of Congress of the 8th August last," and the gold content of the dollar is fixed: a pound troy of gold, eleven parts fine and one part alloy, is equal to "two hundred and nine dollars, seven dimes and seven cents, money of the United States . . . " Not until 1792, however, did the mint become a reality when the Congress authorized its establishment in Philadelphia. This copy is uncut.

352. **UNITED STATES. CONTINENTAL CONGRESS**
An Ordinance for the Government of the Territory of the United States, North-West of the River Ohio.
[New York, 1787]

The Northwest Ordinance provided the authority and the plan by which the western expansion of the United States was accomplished by making provision for the admission of new states. It also established religious freedom, prohibited slavery, and instituted the fundamental New England principle of public education. It, and the important Ordinance of 1785, which provided for the survey and subsequent sale of public lands, were both instruments of the Congress under the Articles of Confederation. They are fundamental documents in American history. This copy includes the integral blank leaf. (Also in the collection are two issues of the printed *Act* of the first Congress (1789) implementing the Ordinance.)

353. **UNITED STATES. TREATIES**
A Treaty of Amity, Commerce, and Navigation, between His Britannick Majesty, and the United States of America.
Philadelphia: Benj. Franklin Bache, [1795]

In 1794 Chief Justice John Jay went to London as Minister Plenipotentiary and Envoy Extraordinary to the Court of St. James's to negotiate a peaceful settlement of Anglo-American differences. "Jay's Treaty"—as it is commonly known—adjusted a series of disputes centering on commercial conflicts, neutral rights, and continuous British occupation of posts in the Old Northwest, contrary to the Treaty of Paris. Signed in London on 19 November 1794, it was not ratified until 1796.

Meanwhile the Treaty was printed in July 1795, without authority, from a copy sent by newly elected Senator Stevens Thomson Mason of Virginia to Bache, "that the people should no longer be left in doubt about it." The rules of the Senate strictly forbade such a violation of secrecy. The Treaty became an issue between the Federalists, who supported it and were generally pro-British, and the emerging Jeffersonian Republicans, who tended to favor Revolutionary France.

354. **UNITED STATES. TREATIES**
By George Washington, President of the United States of America: A Proclamation.
[Philadelphia: Francis Childs, 1796]

After lengthy debate Congress ratified and Washington signed Jay's Treaty on 29 February 1796. This is a copy of the first official edition; the printed certification is signed in manuscript by Timothy Pickering, Secretary of State.

355. **UNITED STATES. TREATIES**
Treaties Made between Great Britain and the United States...
Troy: Parker and Bliss, 1815.

This work contains the Treaty of Paris (1783), Jay's Treaty (1794), the rejected Treaty of 1806 designed to settle outstanding differences with Great Britain, and the Treaty of Ghent (1814) ending the War of 1812. In addition it contains Monroe's letter recommending the ratification of the Treaty of 1806. In this copy, from the collection of Frank C. Deering, is inserted a frontispiece of Monroe taken from a later book.

356. **VIRGINIA. CONVENTION, 1788**
Debates and Other Proceedings of the Convention of Virginia... to Which Is Prefixed, the Federal Constitution.
Petersburg: Hunter and Prentis; William Prentis, 1788–89.
3 vols.

The Virginia Convention, the best prepared of all the ratification conventions, met in Richmond. The advocates and opponents of ratification of the new Constitution, led by James Madison and Patrick Henry respectively, were almost equally divided. Stenographically reported by David Robertson of Petersburg, the *Debates* record the month-long examination of the document. The pro-ratification forces managed to get the Constitution debated clause by clause, a procedure that eventually weakened the effect of Henry's flamboyant oratory. These forces prevailed, agreeing that a bill of rights would be needed after ratification. On 25 June 1788 Virginia became the tenth state to enter the Union. This set is in original boards and uncut.

357. **JOHN A. WAKEFIELD**
History of the War between the United States and the Sac and Fox Nations of Indians...
Jacksonville: Calvin Goody, 1834.

This work is one of the most important contemporary sources on the Black Hawk War and other Indian troubles of the period. For the 1827 campaign, Wakefield used oral reminiscences and newspaper accounts, but in the last two campaigns he was an eyewitness serving as a scout and dispatcher. The Black Hawk War ended in the summer of 1832 when the starving warriors were cornered and, together with women and children, were massacred. Among the militia officers who pursued Chief Black Hawk was the young Captain Abraham Lincoln. This work also contains the original narrative of the Indian captivity of the Hall girls, as related by their elder sister. Wakefield had three thousand copies printed; this copy is bound in original muslin-covered boards.

358. **JOHN A. WAKEFIELD**
History of the War between the United States and the Sac and Fox Nations of Indians . . .
Jacksonville: Calvin Goody, 1834.

Another copy, in contemporary marbled boards with calf spine.

359. **LEW WALLACE**
Ben Hur: A Tale of the Christ.
New York: Harper & Brothers, 1880.

A Hoosier by birth, Wallace served in the Mexican War and the Civil War, and wrote a successful first novel (now entirely forgotten) in 1873. He served as Governor of New Mexico 1878–81, and in 1880 published *Ben Hur,* a romantic depiction of the late Roman Empire and the rise of Christianity. It was an enormous, much translated success, and was later made into two "colossal superspectacle" motion pictures. This is a fine, fresh copy accompanied by a letter to his publisher, dated 6 September 1886, about the book's later reception.

360. **ELBERT WALLER**
Illinois Pioneer Days.
Litchfield, Illinois: E. B. Lewis, 1918.

Published in commemoration of Illinois's centennial as a state, this little booklet gives short descriptions of pioneer ways and institutions and includes a brief vocabulary: "*Drap,* an incorrect pronunciation of drop, e.g., I just drapped in to see you a minute, or, The children drap the corn." It is in its original printed wrappers.

361. **[HORACE WALPOLE]**
The Castle of Otranto . . .
London: Tho. Lownds, 1765.

Famed for his "gothick" house, Strawberry Hill, near Twickenham, and also for his witty and erudite conversation and letters, Walpole wrote one novel. It purports to be a translation "from the original Italian of Onuphrio Muralto, Canon of the Church of St. Nicholas at Otranto," though his authorship was acknowledged in the second edition, published after the success of the first. Like Walpole's house, the story is "gothick," the events taking place in the twelfth and thirteenth centuries. It is the first of the numerous "tales of terror" published mainly from 1780 to 1820. Five hundred copies were published in December 1764; this copy is in contemporary half calf.

362. [GEORGE WASHINGTON]
The Journal of Major George Washington, Sent by the Hon. Robert Dinwiddie, Esq; His Majesty's Lieutenant-Governor, and Commander in Chief of Virginia, to the Commandant of the French Forces in Ohio ...
London: T. Jefferys, 1754.

Although only twenty-one years old, Washington was appointed by Dinwiddie to undertake the difficult mission of proceeding to the Ohio country to demand withdrawal of the French and to strengthen the friendship with the Six Nations. With a party of six frontiersmen, he left Will's Creek on 15 November 1753. Washington endured many hardships on the journey (he nearly died twice on the return trip), but completed his mission and arrived in Williamsburg 16 January 1754. In the preface of his first published work, Washington informs us that "there intervened but one Day between my Arrival in Williamsburg, and the Time for the Council's Meeting, for me to prepare and transcribe, from the rough Minutes I had taken in my Travels, this Journal ... " His report, first printed in Williamsburg, created a sensation and was reprinted quickly in London.

This fine copy of the London edition is stitched and uncut as issued and includes the folding "Map of the Western Parts of the Colony of Virginia, as far as the Mississippi." In the lower right corner, the map reads: "The Shawanons are the same with ye Senekas one of the Six Nations." The original manuscript of the *Journal* is in the Public Record Office in London.

363. **GEORGE WASHINGTON**
A.L.S. to John Jay.
Mount Vernon, 15 April 1788. 1 p.

In this letter to Jay, Washington acknowledges receipt of Volume I of *The Federalist* and expresses his sincere thanks and esteem. Jay had sent Washington Volume I (containing the first thirty-six essays) on 24 March, just two days after it was published.

364. **GEORGE WASHINGTON**
Manuscript Commission Appointing John Jay First Chief Justice of the Supreme Court.
[New York, 1789] 1 p.

Five months after his inauguration as the first President of the United States, Washington signed the Judiciary Act (24 September 1789), providing for the appointment of a Chief Justice and five Associate Justices. He appointed John Jay as the first Chief Justice on 26 September 1789. After serving as the Secretary of Foreign Affairs under the old government from 1784 to 1789, Jay was essentially given his choice of offices by Washington.

The Supreme Court first convened on 1 February 1790 at the Royal Exchange in New York City, then the capital city. Under Jay's administration, the Court concerned itself mostly with establishing procedures for later years. While in office, Jay spent most of 1794 negotiating the treaty with Great Britain which now bears his name. Upon his return to New York City in 1795, he accepted nomination and election as Governor of New York. (A series of letters by Adams, Jay, and Marshall concerning Jay's later renomination as United States Chief Justice, an appointment which he declined, are also in the collection.) This commission is on vellum and is signed by Washington.

365. **[GEORGE WASHINGTON]**
The President's Address to the People of the United States, September 17, 1796, Intimating His Resolution of Retiring from Public Service, When the Present Term of Presidency Expires.
Philadelphia: W. Young, Mills & Son, 1796.

Having given more than twenty-two years of almost continuous service to his country, on 8 May 1796 Washington had written Jay of "the trouble and perplexities which . . . have worn away my mind more than my body; and renders [sic] ease & retirement indispensably necessary to both during the short time I have to stay here." The *Farewell Address*, a monument of American policy, was probably written with the assistance of Hamilton and Madison. An affectionate valedictory to the American people, Washington's *Address* urged the necessity of a strong central government and warned against "the insidious wiles of foreign influence." The *Address* was first published on 19 September 1796 in the Philadelphia newspaper, *Claypole's American Daily Advertiser*. It was immediately reprinted, under various titles, in dozens of pamphlet editions. This edition, advertised in *Fenno's Gazette* on Wednesday evening, 21 September 1796, is one of the earliest.

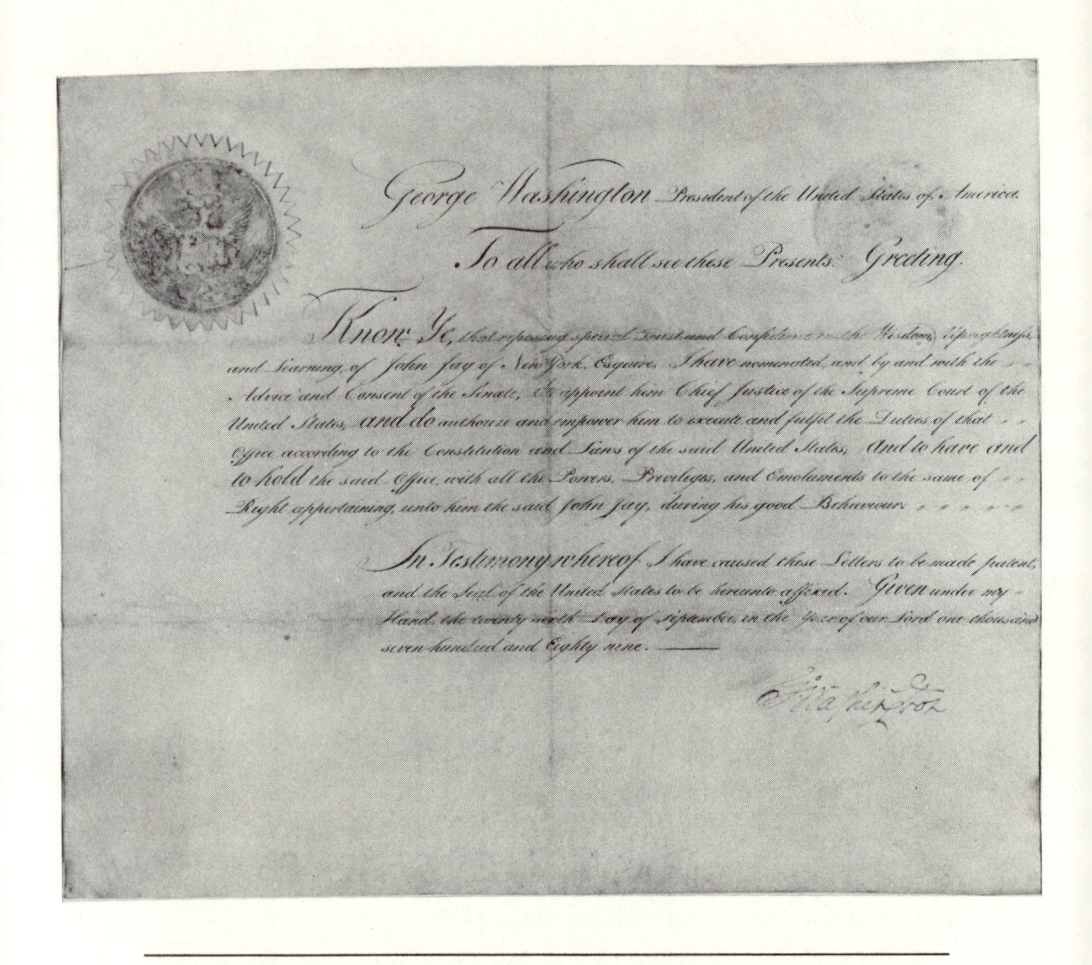

364. George Washington, Manuscript Commission Appointing John Jay First Chief Justice of the Supreme Court (1789)

366. **DANIEL WEBSTER**
A Discourse in Commemoration of the Lives and Services of John Adams and Thomas Jefferson, Delivered in Faneuil Hall, Boston, August 2, 1826.
Boston: Cummings, Hilliard, 1826.

The deaths of Adams and Jefferson within a few hours of each other on 4 July 1826, the fiftieth anniversary of the Declaration of Independence, caused a great national mourning. Daniel Webster, the most famous orator of the time, delivered this *Discourse* at the request of the Boston City Council. Webster concludes, "WASHINGTON is in the clear, upper sky. These other stars have now joined the American constellation; they circle round their centre, and the heavens beam with new light." Accompanied by the separate "Order of Exercises," the *Discourse* is in original paper wrappers and inscribed "Joseph Hall Esq. with the best regards of the Author." Hall, a native of Massachusetts, was later congressman from Maine.

367. **NOAH WEBSTER**
A Compendious Dictionary of the English Language.
Hartford: Hudson & Goodwin; New-Haven: Increase Cooke, 1806.

Webster's publishing career was launched with his famous *Spelling Book* (1783–85). There followed periods of teaching, legal practice, and journalism, but he returned in 1803 to his first love, linguistic scholarship. Webster was "a born definer of words," according to Sir James Murray, the editor of the *Oxford English Dictionary*, and produced in 1806 his duodecimo *Compendious Dictionary*, the forerunner of his most ambitious work, *An American Dictionary of the English Language* (1828). While compiling the present work, Webster learned the technique of lexicography, and he experimented with new methods. For example, he added 5,000 words not included in previous dictionaries and began to record "Americanisms" and to advocate American spellings. His efforts had an enormous impact on nineteenth-century public education. Laid in is a leaf of manuscript by Webster analyzing the correct usage of certain words.

368. **[GILBERT WHITE]**
The Natural History and Antiquities of Selborne, in the County of Southampton.
London: B. White and Son, 1789.

Educated at Oriel College, Oxford, White spent most of his life as curate of Selborne in Hampshire, refusing other opportunities in order to remain in his beloved birthplace. He early showed evidence of the observant naturalist's bent. The long correspondence he began in 1767 with two distinguished naturalists, Thomas Pennant and Daines Barrington, formed the basis of his *The Natural History and Antiquities of Selborne,* published four years before his death; it soon became an English classic. The natural beauty and perennial charm of this work are due in part to the fact that, as James Russell Lowell observed, "open the book where you will, it takes you out of doors." This uncut copy is in original marbled boards.

369. **WALT WHITMAN**
Leaves of Grass.
Brooklyn, 1855.

"Practically everything that can be said about the significance of this book has been said by its author, and most of it is true." These poems are saturated with the "vehemence of pride and audacity of freedom necessary to loosen the mind of still-to-be-form'd America from the folds, the superstitions, and all the long, tenacious, and European past." Whitman is the poet and prophet of democracy and the forerunner of modern verse; his "barbaric yawp" was recognized at the time not least by Emerson in his famous salutation, and it continues to echo to this day. This is a copy of the first issue in a brilliant and immaculate binding.

370. **WALT WHITMAN**
Leaves of Grass . . .
Philadelphia: David McKay, 1891–'2.

Whitman kept revising and enlarging *Leaves of Grass* all his life, publishing ten editions, each of which is virtually a new work. This, the so-called Death-Bed Edition, is the last edition prepared under his supervision; it includes three annexes. Whitman's intimate friend and later his chronicler, Horace Traubel, had a few advance copies (not more than fifty) specially bound to show Whitman, who was very ill at the time and anxious to see it. Some of them Whitman sent to special friends: this is one of those, in rough paper wrappers with a yellow printed label. It is inscribed to the English critic: "To Edward Dowden, Jan. 7, 1892, sent by Walt Whitman from his sick bed. H[orace] L. T[raubel], Camden." Whitman died on 26 March 1892.

371. **JOHN GREENLEAF WHITTIER**
Snow-Bound: A Winter Idyll.
Boston: Ticknor and Fields, 1866.

Whittier, the Quaker poet, was as popular as Longfellow in the nineteenth century, owing to the transparent sincerity and nobility of his character and to the appeal of his ballads. *Snow-Bound,* a description of an old Puritan colonial interior, had a great success and was read aloud around the fireplace by several generations. This copy, in green cloth, is of the first issue.

372. **PRINCE MAXIMILIAN OF WIED**
Travels in the Interior of North America.
London: Ackermann, 1843–44. 1 vol. and atlas of plates.

Between 4 July 1832 and 16 July 1834 German Prince Maximilian of Wied and Swiss artist Karl Bodmer pushed deeply into the American wilderness, spending much of their time in the Indian country of the Upper Missouri. Under contract to the experienced naturalist, Bodmer executed magnificent watercolors to illustrate Maximilian's written observations of their historic journey that covered some ten thousand miles.

After his return to Germany, Maximilian published his narration in German along with a folio atlas of colored plates prepared by Bodmer based on his watercolors. Maximilian's and Bodmer's written and visual record of the western frontier in the early 1830's has long been regarded as one of the most important accounts of the Great Plains Indians before encounter with whites irrevocably changed their culture; it remains a fundamental source for the study of that time and place. This, the most complete English translation, includes a folding map illustrating the route and the *Atlas,* after Bodmer's watercolors, containing 81 plates, 64 of which are devoted to Indian life.

373. **EDWARD WIGGLESWORTH**
Calculations on American Population . . .
Boston: John Boyle, 1775.

Educator and theologian, Wigglesworth graduated from Harvard College in 1749 and remained there as resident scholar. His *Calculations on American Population* discusses the annual increase of inhabitants in the colonies, and he estimated that "British Americans," as he calls them, would increase to one and a half billion by the end of the twentieth century. He also noted that of a total population of approximately three million in 1775, more than half a million were slaves—"to the disgrace of America slavery still prevails here."

374. **ROGER WILLIAMS**
A Key into the Language of America; or, An Help to the Languages of the Natives in That Part of America, Called New-England.
London: Gregory Dexter, 1643.

Written by the founder of Rhode Island while on board ship to London, this is the first serious attempt to record the vocabulary of the native language of the Massachusetts and neighboring Indians. In the preface he states, "I drew the *materialls* in a rude lumpe at Sea, as a private *helpe* to my owne memory, that I might not by my present absence *lightly lose* what I had so *dearely bought* in some few yeares *hardship,* and *charges* among the *Barbarians.*"

The book consists of a series of classified vocabularies, and is in fact the first Indian-English dictionary other than brief vocabularies. Scattered through the work are observations on the native inhabitants and their surroundings. On the flyleaf is written, "I had this Book from Benjamin Franklin of Philadelphia. Minister from the United States of America at the court of Versailles. [In another hand:] E: Poore." In this copy the title page has been mounted.

375. **NATHANIEL PARKER WILLIS**
Trenton Falls, Picturesque and Descriptive . . .
New York: George P. Putnam, 1851.

Trenton Falls, in Oneida County, New York, is described as being "the most *enjoyably beautiful* spot, among the resorts of romantic scenery in our country." The original description was written by the Rev. John Sherman and published in 1827; to this, Willis, the well-known editor and writer, has added further material to bring it up to date. There are a number of illustrations after wood-engravings by Nathaniel Orr.

376. **WOODROW WILSON**
The State . . .
Boston: D. C. Heath, 1889.

After giving up his clientless law practice in 1883, Wilson entered Johns Hopkins University to study government and history, receiving his Ph.D. degree in 1886. He was called to Wesleyan University in 1888 as professor of history and political economy. While there he published this comprehensive textbook in political science. Almost seven hundred pages in length, it discusses the evolution and character of governments from classical times to the present. This copy is inscribed "Mrs. Adam J. Begges, With the sincere affection of her nephew, Woodrow Wilson, Oct. 1889."

377. **WOODROW WILSON**
Constitutional Government in the United States.
New York: The Columbia University Press, 1908.

Written while Wilson was president of Princeton, this was one of the Columbia University Lecture Series. The front flyleaf is inscribed: "The constitution of the United States, like the constitution of every living state, grows and is altered by force of circumstances and changes in affairs. The effect of a written constitution is only to render the growth more subtle, more studious, more conservative, more of a thing of carefully, almost unconsciously, wrought sequences. Our statesmen must, in the midst of origination, have the spirit of lawyers. Woodrow Wilson. Princeton, 18 Oct., '09." This fine, fresh copy was formerly in the A. Edward Newton collection.

378. **WOODROW WILSON**
T.L.S. to Herbert Bruce Brougham.
Paris, 17 December 1918. 1 p.

In a letter written the previous day (a typed and signed copy of which is present) Brougham had urged the President to continue to press for a democratic League of Nations and warned him of the difficult forces opposing him. Wilson responds that he is aware of such forces and that "I will stand fast to the principles and purposes which I have avowed."

379. **OWEN WISTER**
The Virginian: A Horseman of the Plains.
New York and London: Macmillan, 1902.

Member of a prominent Pennsylvania family, Wister was graduated from Harvard *summa cum laude* in 1882. On the advice of his physician, he went west to Wyoming for several summers and found there the subject matter to start a literary career. Wister's last western novel, *The Virginian* centered on the Wyoming cowpunchers of the 1870's and 1880's and established many of the patterns for modern western fiction. Dedicated to his classmate Theodore Roosevelt, the novel was an instant success and remains popular today.

380. **MARY WOLLSTONECRAFT**
A Vindication of the Rights of Woman . . .
London: J. Johnson, 1792.

After an unhappy childhood, Wollstonecraft, an impulsive and enthusiastic woman, pursued several occupations: schoolteacher, governess, and reader for Joseph Johnson, her eventual publisher. Written in six weeks, *A Vindication of the Rights of Woman* was a courageous and radical attack on the conventions of the day. Wollstonecraft's central theme, the illumination of woman's mind, was argued with a vigorous freedom of speech which caused deep offense: "Marriage will never be held sacred till women, by being brought up with men, are prepared to be their companions rather than their mistresses." She later lived with the American soldier and writer Gilbert Imlay, and subsequently with William Godwin, whom she married. Her work is now regarded as a landmark of feminism. This copy is in original boards and uncut.

381. JOHN WOODS
Two Years' Residence in the Settlement of the English Prairie...
London: Longman, Hurst, Rees, Orme, and Brown, 1822.

Woods, a well-to-do English farmer, settled on the "English Prairie" in southeastern Illinois in 1819. This account of his journey to the Illinois country and his residence there (1819–21) provides an interesting and favorable view of the social life and conditions of the time. In the section on vegetable productions, Woods describes the cultivation of corn, "the most important article of the country's growth," in great detail. He notes that "they also plant a small kind of French-bean with part of their corn, the stalks serving instead of sticks for the beans to run on." He also presents much valuable information about social, economic, and political conditions in other parts of the state.

382. JOHN PETER ZENGER
The Case and Tryal of John Peter Zenger, of New-York, Printer...
London: J. Wilford, 1750.

Zenger's polemical articles and rhymes caused him to be arrested in November 1734 and tried for seditious libel in 1735 after his newspaper, *The New-York Weekly Journal,* had attacked Governor William Crosby. (Also in the collection is a two-year run of the *Journal.*) In the trial, Zenger was brilliantly defended by Andrew Hamilton, who established the principle that in prosecutions of libel the jury are the judges of both the law and the facts of a case. Zenger, "the morning star of liberty," was acquitted after spending nearly ten months in prison. The verdict of this case became the first major victory for the freedom of the press in the American colonies.

Soon after his acquittal, Zenger printed a complete verbatim account of the trial in his newspaper. The report, first published separately in 1736, was probably prepared by James Alexander, one of Zenger's counsel. The case aroused much interest in the colonies and Great Britain, and the work was reprinted in numerous editions. This is one of the later London editions.